THREAD IN THE LOOM

THREAD IN THE LOOM:
ESSAYS ON AFRICAN
LITERATURE AND CULTURE

NIYI OSUNDARE

Africa World Press, Inc.

P.O. Box 1892
Trenton, NJ 08607

P.O. Box 48
Asmara, ERITREA

Africa World Press, Inc.

P.O. Box 1892
Trenton, NJ 08607

P.O. Box 48
Asmara, ERITREA

Copyright © 2002 Niyi Osundare

First Printing 2002

Cover artwork: untitled by Moyo Ogundipe
Cover design: Ashraful Haque
Book design: Getahun Seyoum Alemayehu and 'Damola Ifaturoti

Library of Congress Cataloging-in-Publication Data

Osundare, Niyi, 1947-
    Thread in the loom : essays on African literature and culture / Niyi Osundare
      p. cm.
    Includes bibliographical references and index.
    ISBN 0-86543-865-X -- ISBN 0-86543-866-8 (pbk.)
    1. African literature--Political aspects. 2. African literature--Social aspects. 3. Literature and society--Africa. 4. Nigerian literature--Political aspects. 5. Nigerian literature--Social aspects. 6. Literature and society--Nigeria. 7. Osundare, Niyi, 1947---Political and social views. I. Title.

PL8010. O76 2000
809'.896--dc21

00-034865

To

Bayo Ogunjimi

Claude Ake
&
Frank Uche Mowah

....in memoriam

APPRECIATION

I would like to express my gratitude to: the College of Liberal Arts, University of New Orleans for the 1998 research grant which helped the preparation of this book; the Centre of West African Studies, The University of Birmingham, U.K., for the 1995 Cadbury Fellowship; Iwalewa Haus, University of Bayreuth, Germany, for a brief research residency in 1996; and the University of Ibadan, Nigeria, whose resources facilitated many of the essays in this book.

Contents

ACKNOWLEDGEMENTS

The author and the publisher would like to thank the following for permission to use material in this book.

African Literature Association Bulletin, Vol.24, No.2, 1998; *Presence Africaine,* No. 158, 2nd Semester, 1998, for "Freedom and the Creative Space"

Goshen College, Indiana, U.S.A. Convocation Lecture Series, 1988; *African Literature Association Bulletin*, Vol. 15, No. 4, 1989, for "Stubborn Thread in the Loom of Being: The Writer as Memory of the World".

Olusegun Oladipo, Editor, *Remaking Africa: Challenges of the Twenty First Century*. Ibadan, Nigeria:Hope Publications, 1998, for "Squaring up to Africa's Future: A Writer's Reflections on the Problems of a Continent".

West Africa, 9-15 December, 1991; *Literatur Nachrichten*, Nr. 32, Jan-Marz, 1992; *Glendora Review*, Vol.1, No.4, 1996, for "Of Prizes and Messiahs".

Dialogue in African Philosophy Monograph Series, Ibadan, Nigeria, 1993, for "African Literature and the Crisis of Post-Structuralist Theorising"; also in *Matatu*, 1995, under the title "How Post-Colonial is African Literature?"

Anglistentag: Proceedings of the Conference of the German Association of University Professors of English, 1997, for "Singers of a New Dawn: Nigerian Literature from the Second Generation on".

Newswatch, November 18, 1996; *African Literature Association Bulletin*, Vol. 23, No. 1, 1997, for "The Longest Day".

The Guardian (Nigeria), July 1996, for "The Travails of Efficiency"

The Centre of West African Studies, University of Birmingham, U.K., for "Yoruba Thought, English Words: a Poet's Journey Through the Tunnel of Two Tongues".

L'universite de Toulouse-le Mirail; *Anglophonia Caliban*, No. 7, Universite de Toulouse-Le Mirail, January 2000, for "Thresholds and Millennial Crossings".

The Herald (Harare), August 1991; West Africa, 7-13 October, 1991; *Literatur Nachrichten*, Nr. 31, Oktober-Dezember, 1991; Don Burness, Editor, *Echoes of the Sunbird*. Ohio University Monographs in International Studies, Africa Series, No. 62, 1993, for "The Possibilities of Hope".

PREFACE

The short piece, "Behold the Feast, but Where is the Guest?",
included in this selection, owes its provenance to a context
which I consider important for the understanding of the purpose,
mission, and vision of the other essays. It was my opening
address at the British Council Exhibition on West African
Writers in celebration of Wole Soyinka's 60th birthday, which
took place at the Nigerian Institute of International Affairs in
Lagos on June 19, 1995. A few days before, I had accepted the
assignment with a somewhat historic sense of mission, for the
exhibition came up just weeks after Soyinka had been forced into
exile by General Sanni Abacha's murderous dictatorship. In a
frenzy that would make the Inquisition look like a liberal
funfare, a virulent, systematic war had commenced on Soyinka
and his works, his friends and associates. It was a war so base, so
shocking in its jejune perversity that even school children were
forbidden to talk openly about the Soyinka text on their reading
list, or put a Soyinka play on their stage. We thought it was only
a matter of time for a decree to be out making public mention of
Soyinka's name a treasonable offence!

So I was hardly surprised to see the meagre turnout at the exhibition. The organisers (who must be commended for their courage in those circumstances) had decided not to publicize the event for fear of its disruption by government security agents. It was also perilously close to the June 12* anniversary with all the fury and phobia it had generated in the Abacha era. But what the gathering lacked in quantity, it more than made up for in the quality of its commitment and insight. We seized that moment and talked about the state of our literature, our country, our world, our silence.

Silence and the battle against it: these are the common threads in the loom of these essays, their triggering principle, their *raison d'etre*. And I am talking here of that kind of silence which is not just the flip side of speech, but its negator and executioner, a hush cloud fomented by tyrants of all kinds, enforced by all kinds of method and madness. In the tainted universe of this silence, no healthy exchange is possible; no other voice is allowed in the public arena besides the dictator's metallic roar. Needless to say, literature, that preeminent offspring of verbal exchange, is tyranny's prime victim—but also its ultimate nemesis.

The Nigerian situation mentioned above replicates itself with mortifying frequency in other parts of Africa, a condition which is not only an indication of Africa's underdevelopment, but is also a prominent cause of that malaise. However, these essays enjoin us to see Africa's silence in its internal dimensions without losing sight of those potent factors which affect the continent from distances beyond its shores. For even in this era of triumphal globalization, Africa still hangs on to a precarious existence in what used to be the margin, but which right now can be more appropriately described as the margin of the margin, a zone of abysmal silence and disarticulation, stripped of agency and talk-back capability. Even on this threshold of a new millennium, the continent remains invisible on the map of a global village drawn by those who control the pencil as well as the paper. The practice of unequal exchange so methodically highlighted by social scientists in the socio-economic relations between Africa and the industrialized parts of the world is equally pernicious at the cultural-literary level. In an age of "travelling theories" and "travelling texts", externally generated ideas—and prejudices—travel with imperial ease and confidence in Africa, whereas the "canon war" makes it extremely difficult for African texts to make it to the reading list of many European and American institutions.

Transnational publishing companies and their octopal distribution networks, foreign media organizations with their awesome reach and power, impact virtually every household on the continent with monologic impunity, virtually drowning out indigenous voices. African texts and ideas, hobbled by myriad historical and contemporary disabilities, have no access to the passport which guarantees such peripatetic prerogatives. Thus the world talks to (or at) Africa, but takes little or nothing in reply by way of the continent's own ideas and responses. And so a battery of nagging questions arises: whose ideas are designed and packaged to rule the world? Who decides what should be heard and what should not? What can be done to change this state of unequal discourse and bring a measure of reciprocity to the cultural traffic between Africa and the rest of the world? How can the signifying field be made more level? What should be done to amplify Africa's voice above its enforced silence? These are some of the questions raised in these essays. They are by no means new, but I think they will continue to pester our consciousness (if not our conscience) until they get the answers which they so urgently need—and deserve. For until that time, high-sounding, powerfully hyped mantras such as "one world", "global village", "global network", "international information super highway", "multiculturalism", etc would be seen to contain more wind than wisdom. As the Yoruba say, Ajọjẹ o dun b'ẹni kan o ni (The feast cannot be enjoyable if some of the partakers are not able to contribute).

The problems facing Africa are many, deep-seated and far-reaching. Many African writers have dared these monsters at grave risk to their freedom and, in some cases, their lives. In our present circumstances, the text cannot be the only thing nor can the author afford to be "dead", unless, of course, like Ken Saro Wiwa ("The Longest Day"), s/he is killed by an evil junta mortally scared of her/his existence. This book contains a selection from my essays and addresses on different occasions and on diverse topics over a period of twelve years, on literature, language, the arts, and wider social issues. Running through them is my abiding concern with the necessity of memory and remembrance, freedom, justice (local and global, in all its ramifications), the indispensability of hope, and the need to widen the creative space by re-humanizing the world.

Literature matters not only because it provides us with diversion and pleasure, but also because it creates positive dreams which can serve as alternative—and antidote—to our pervasive nightmare. From its very beginnings, African literature has kept up its role as the thread in Africa's loom of being, enrobing the continent's thoughts, creating a fiction which enriches and constantly interrogates its fact, making sure that Africa does not go into the next millennium still mute, naked, and forlornly cold.

- The date of Nigeria's freest and fairest presidential election, whose annulment by the military in June 1993 precipitated a chain of national crises.

·FREEDOM AND THE CREATIVE SPACE

In my preface to *Great Africans on Record: A Dictionary of African Quotations* by the Nigerian journalist Victor Omuabor, I reached this general but painful conclusion: "Africa today is a dangerous place to think, a risky place to argue". I was led to this verdict not only by the virtual absence of human rights on the continent, but also by the harrowing irony created by the book itself. For here is a compendium of the contemplations of African luminaries on a wide variety of subjects, issues, and ideas. And, naturally, a substantial portion of these come from the continent's political rulers—civilian and military. And how eloquent they wax on burning issues such as human rights, freedom and liberty, social justice, the dignity of the human person, and the necessity of a vision! Eloquent proverbs; diligent aphorisms with an apt, epigrammatic intensity. And then you ask: how can such beautiful thoughts come from rulers who have made Africa so ugly? How can rulers who talk about freedom with such robust piety haul critics and opponents into jail or send dissident writers to the gallows with such medieval equanimity?

The gulf between thought and action in contemporary Africa is so pathologically wide that one is constrained to wonder if the time has not come to charge our rulers' ghost writers with aiding and abetting criminal hypocrisy! We should be convinced beyond any unreasonable doubt now that in Africa today, rulers who combine thought and action are tragically few and far between. Some who have attempted to achieve this balance and thereby proceed from rulership to leadership, have always had their tenures, if not their lives, cut short by those who profit from Africa's mess. Is anyone still wondering, then, why the continent has not had its fair share of "philosopher-kings"? Permit me to poach once again from said preface:

> Philosopher-kings never thrive in a moral and social vacuum. If this calibre of rulers is lamentably small in Africa today, it is because more often than not, the kings of modern African nation-states usurp the kingship without the humanizing temper of its complementary philosophy. The murderous dictators and presidents-for-life who populate Africa's political landscape are not only incapable of generating ideas that are valid across time and place; they are, naturally, hostile to such ideas and even more, to those who have the audacity to be their authors.[1]

This is why Africa remains the misery region of the world, a dinosaur left panting in the wilderness while the vanguard of humanity is busy exploring the possibilities of Mars and Saturn. The pogroms in Rwanda, the anarchy in Somalia, the political musical chairs in Sierra Leone and the Congo, the flashpoints of Nigeria, Algeria, and Kenya, the uneasy peace in Angola, the spasmodic rumbles from other parts of Africa... all bleeding historical wounds which defy a facile balm and insist on total healing.

But can healing really take place at the present moment, in the present circumstances—without first clearing up the political mess? In virtually all parts of Africa, the superstition of power is stronger than the science of responsibility. Our people, so long brutalized by the monsters of slavery and colonialism, are still daily humiliated and dehumanized by "indigenous" governments they did not elect, by rulers who rule by the brutal logic of the gun, and who hang on to power by systematically violating their countries and weakening the glue in their crevices through a divide-and-rule design to keep themselves in power. To such rulers, dissent is treason; to assay an alternative vision is to run foul of the tyrant's despotic blindness. Only statesmen that are human can recognize and respect the human rights of others. Only leaders whose desire for power has been tempered by wisdom and refinement can respect the sanctity of the ballot and the inviolability of the people's collective will.

But democracy, the rule of the rational and popular will of the people, remains in constant jeopardy in Africa: an awkward alien in some parts, a warped, corrupted imposition in many, and a treasonable taboo in others. Where else except in Africa and those other parts of the globe relegated as the "Third World" would the military annul a free and fair election, dump the popular winner in gaol, while continuing to clamp their iron rule on a people so sorely tired of their yoke? As I have said several times before, the bane of Africa's development is her misfortune of always having the wrong rulers at the right time, rulers who bring out the worst in our people, rulers who measure their Lilliputian height by the genuflection of those they rule.

The repercussions of this state of repression for the creative spirit are incalculable. One of its crucial casualties is freedom. As we all know, freedom is as vital to the creative enterprise as oxygen is to a living organism. That enterprise can only flower and flourish when the creative spirit has the liberty to dare, venture, argue, make mistakes, lose and discover itself in the rapture of being and becoming. It can only flourish when it has the liberty to contemplate (for the spirit that can contemplate is one that can anticipate), ruminate, brood, dream, navigate the threshold of madness (not insanity!), develop inner eyes for seeing and apprehending unborn possibilities, cultivate the audacity to keep telling the emperor: "Your Majesty, thou, indeed, art naked". The art and act of creation need a certain latitude, a certain space in which even the sky is too low as an upper limit.

Let us seek illustration in a few conventional instances. Would Isaac Newton have been able to distill the gravitational theory from the mundane physics of a fallen apple if his wondering mind had been split between scientific contemplation and a debilitating dread of the sword of state? Would Albert Einstein have taken Newton's findings to new heights if his laboratory was a battleground for frequent ransacks by state security agents in their endless search for "subversive material"? Take a look at traditional Africa prior to the coming of alien predators and their native successors. Consider the beauty and philosophical amplitude of our proverbs and idioms, the "truthful lie" of our riddles, jokes, fables, and tales; the lyrical gravity of our poetry. Could these collective wisdoms have emerged in societies terrorized by the thought police and the Mephistophelian guardians of state prisons? The freedom to stand and stare is basic to any creative leap. Unfortunately, that is a state of existence that is in peril virtually everywhere in Africa today. And so the conscientious writer has to keep looking over her/his shoulders, waiting for the next knock on the door, considering with mortal awe the kind of adjective that should go with her/his noun.

From all angles, the writer is confronted by the terror of deterrence. A state which parades prisons full of writers and graves littered with the bones of visionary thinkers and activists is telling prospective writers and thinkers in no unmistakable terms: "Behold these, therefore, and learn; do what they have done and suffer their fate." A personal testimony will elucidate my point here. As part of the activities marking my 50th Birthday last year, my old play, *The State Visit*, a clearly anti-fascist satire, was put on stage. There were symposia and readings based on my works; and the Nigerian media gave me generous coverage. As interview after interview appeared in the media, re-affirming my opposition to military rule and my abiding faith in democracy, warnings and admonitions started coming from former classmates, colleagues, friends, and family: "Gently, gently o. Don't abuse government o. See what they did to Kunle Ajibade and George Mbah. See what they did to Ken Saro Wiwa....Please, gently, gently o..."

Of course, only a fool or one practically insane could have ignored such warnings or dismissed them as timid remonstrations of faint-hearted relations. As one who had lived in Nigeria for 50 years, I knew where those warnings were coming from. But I also reassured my concerned friends that I was not suffering from a martyr syndrome, that mine was not so much the abuse of government as the abuse of the abuse of governance, an indictment of those who put the gun between us and our rights, of those who keep us trapped in Medieval darkness, of those who, now or in the past, have turned our potentially great country into the laughing stock of the world. Like the Painter in *The State Visit*, I gave the assurance that my loyalty is to our country, its people, its future, rather than to the transient occupiers of the political throne.

The import of the above experience is clear: every tyranny seeks accomplices in fear and induced silence. Or to put it more accurately, silence induced by fear. All voices of life, of goodness, of vision, are muted so that the tyrant's iron voice can go unchallenged. Public truth is suppressed so as to give official falsehood a monopoly of the airwaves. Tyranny is averse to argument; its megaphone can only blare on one track. It is scared of joining issues because it is mortally scared of the fragility and ephemerality of its own methods. So, what it lacks in intellectual amplitude and social and spiritual legitimacy, it tries to make up for in the overwhelming physicality of its weapons and strategies of violence.

And how can literature help to conquer that fear, rupture that silence, and neutralize that violence? By constantly, intelligently exposing the lie which lies at the root of every violence; the lie which feeds and strengthens it. For as Alexander Solzhenitsyn has very pointedly put it,

> violence can only exist with the help of the lie. Between these two there is a most intimate, natural and fundamental connection. Violence can only be concealed by the lie, and the lie can only be maintained by violence. Any man who has once proclaimed violence as his method is inevitably forced to take the lie as his principle[2]

Now let us enter an important caveat here and do some soul searching. Violence and the lie are not the exclusive vices of tyrants and dictators. History and contemporary happenings have shown that every tyrant has her/his own pool of court poets, praise-singers, hagiographers, and other hack writers—swarming maggots in the royal corpse. They encounter hunger in the streets and pass it off as religious abstinence; they hear clamorous songs of protest and tell their masters it is the national anthem. They slander fellow writers who are in prison, and invent clever justifications for the murder of a colleague on the gallows. There is no evil too outrageous for them to rationalize, no tyrant too monstrous for them to serve. Their eyes, like those of their masters/mistresses, are buried deep in their stomachs.

Every age, every country, has its own share of these writers, but it is to our eternal benefit —and relief—that they are few, and their impact is as short-lived as their vision. The history of the struggle for liberty has been substantially influenced by writers who stay close to the heartbeat and conscience of humanity. Writers who explode the tyrant's myth of invincibility by helping the people out of their sense of helplessness. As natives of the most dehumanized, most flagrantly exploited continent in the world, African writers have never nursed any doubt about the role of art in the struggle for the restoration of human dignity and justice, about the need to widen the space for our dreams and deeds. At no time is that spirit of commitment more necessary than now. Our continent remains, even in this era of "multiparty democracy" and "trade liberalization", the graveyard of liberty and freedom (in the widest sense of those words). Some of our best minds are in prison; many have been forced into internal exile at home or external exile abroad where they eke out a living in what is looking more and more like the second phase of Africa's slavery.

But the pen must till the land; its ink must water the field for the seeds of freedom to germinate, take root, flower, and fruit. Times like these call for a re-affirmation of our commitment to Life through Art; a re-validation of our belief in the inevitability of change and the possibility of hope. According to a Yoruba saying, *"Ibaa togun odun t'eke ti nsare lo, ojo kan pere l'ooto o le ba"* (Let the lie run for twenty years; it will take the truth only one day to overtake it). Art is that truth; the oppressor's violence and its enabling falsehoods constitute the lie. This conviction finds expression in the following poem to Festus Iyayi, the

Nigerian novelist and steadfast Human Rights activist whose radical fervor and skepticism provided me with more than food for thought a couple of years age:

> History
> is an actor
> in a room
> with a thousand mirrors
>
> And so
> Tyranny may be long,
> History is
> always
>
> l
> o
> n
> g
> e
> r^3

The 20th century met Africa in thralldom, a continent cut up like free booty for possession by different imperial powers. It has been one hundred years of struggle and betrayal, of few gains and many failures. As that century hastens to a close, many parts of Africa are still trapped in varying stages of unfreedom. We must get the 21st century to sing a different song. If the out-going century embraced the struggle for independence, the in-coming one must be declared the Century of Democracy and Human Rights (CEDEHURI)—a century that will have no place whatsoever for dictators—benign or malignant, military or civilian. We writers must not relent in our push for that ideal. For we can only hope to widen and secure the creative space by liberating and humanizing the social and political arena. Concerning the 21st century, Africa must borrow a song from Margaret Walker and proclaim for all the world to hear: THIS IS MY CENTURY.

---

* A slightly modified version of the Acceptance Speech for the Fonlon-Nichols Award, Austin, Texas, U.S.A., March 26, 1998.

Notes

1. Victor Omuabor, *Great Africans on Record: A Dictionary of African Quotations*. Lagos, Nigeria: Self published, 1995, p. iii.
2. Alexander Solzhenitsyn, *Nobel Prize Lecture*. London, U.K: Stenvalley Press, 1970, p. 53.
3. Niyi Osundare, *Horses of Memory*. Ibadan, Nigeria:*Heinemann* Educational Books, 1998, p. 115.

*STUBBORN THREAD IN THE LOOM OF BEING:
THE WRITER AS MEMORY OF THE WORLD

During the official launch of *Moonsongs*, my latest volume of poetry, in July this year, a literary journalist with one of Nigeria's newspapers asked me what my overall purpose as a writer is. My answer? To make the world a smaller place: to shrink up the sundering seas, level all intruding mountains, bridge all gulfs, put a lamp in every tunnel. To write in such a way that every speaking mouth will find a listening ear. To make the world so small that every human being irrespective of race, creed, sex, and age will stand tall and proud in it. Above all, to remind humanity of the tortuous, avoidably oppressive journey so far, and make sure it does not forget.

Tall dreams. Lofty projections. I can already hear critics asking me to come down from my castle in the air. For how can one risk such dreams in a world so scared of idealism, a world where humanist ethos are becoming a faint echo, where to be optimistic is to risk being tagged a soppy sentimentalist, a world, above all, where the writer can no longer remind humanity of some crooked paths taken because he has himself lost his memory.

And yet, a writer without memory is like an alphabet without its letters, or a face without a nose. For, needless to say, it is memory which grounds us in history, the root which feeds the manifold branches of human experience. And as the grand old griot has observed in the epic of Sundiata, "whoever knows the history of a country can read its future."[1] It is one with such knowledge that can ask like the Nigerian novelist Chinua Achebe: Where exactly did the rain begin to beat us?" And unless we are awake enough to ask such a question, we may not know where to dry our clothes.

But haven't we overstated our case here? Can anyone still remain a writer, who is afflicted with acute amnesia, the type we are talking about here? How then can his noun find its verb in the syntax of human experience? The fact is that memory is a complex phenomenon whose degree and intensity vary from writer to writer. Very broadly we can distinguish between passive memory which is basically a reservoir of impressions, mostly residual, mostly dormant, retained by the individual or community, and active memory which is those impressions in dynamic recall. The second category shares the same borders with remembrance, the enabling correlative of memory. Both categories find transitive matrix in the act of reminding. For it is hardly enough for the writer merely to have memory or be able to remember; he must also be able to remind. Here begins the writer's affective journey, here the alpha of his historic mission.

But as Hamidou Kane has warned in his intriguingly philosophical novel *Ambiguous Adventure*, a complexly complementary relationship exists between memory and oblivion: "Can one learn this without forgetting that, and is what one learns worth what one forgets?"[2]

Individual memory, like individual life, is finite; communal or social memory is longer, frequently more reliable. But even in both cases, the homeostatic operation mentioned by Kane still exists: old memories fade away, yielding place to new ones. It has always been man's nagging puzzle to find an experiential equilibrium between what to remember and what to forget, and to make sure that the communal baby is not thrown out with the bath water or oblivion. To be sure, the computer, one of man's most versatile and useful inventions, is waging a vigorous war on oblivion through its astounding capacity for memory storage and its equally incredible facility of recall. But that silicon miracle is still man's invention, can only respond to stimuli transmitted to it by man; it can only remember what its human programmer wants it to remember. In other words, the computer can only be a useful (and a powerfully useful one at that!) extension of the human brain; it can never serve as its substitute. The computer can only be a storer of history, it cannot record it in the real sense of the word; it cannot create history and be created by it in the same dialectical way that man can. The computer, therefore, may heal oblivion, it cannot cure amnesia.

All this is not to say that human memory is perfect. Far from it. So many obstacles litter the road between memory and remembering, and between these two and the faculty of reminding. The most virulent of these obstacles are memory manipulation and selective remembrance. Thus, depending upon his prejudices, biases, even fixations, a writer may talk about history of the Christian Church without mentioning the Reformation, about the direction of modern political economy without mentioning Karl Marx, about the Second World War without mentioning the Holocaust, or indeed, the present socio-economic dominance of the Western World without reference to so many centuries of slavery, colonialism and imperialism. Without doubt, one of the principal sources of tension in the present world is the fact that at any given moment, some segments of humanity are busily trying to forget what other segments are arduously striving to remember.

But when we talk so ardently of the unpastness of the past, about its enigmatically intrusive presence, why does literature so readily come to our mind? It does so because literature endures. From classical times to the present, various minds have ceaselessly pointed out the humanistic potential of literature, its ability to create alternative realities, to push further the frontiers of quotidian actuality through a relentless thrust of fresh imagination, its ability to create new answers for old questions, and pose new questions for old answers, its concern for beauty, for the harmonious elevation of the human spirit, and, therefore, its capacity for "seducing" us from ugliness, for healing rifts and stifling fragmentations.

The Romans saw the poet as vates, a prophet figure capable of envisioning elusive futures through the crystal ball of resplendent words; the Renaissance imagination of Phillip Sidney put the poet well above the philosopher and the historian in the competition for idealizable truth; the Romantics voted him in through Shelley as the unacknowledged legislator of mankind, while Matthew Arnold's Victorian voice stressed the need to re-align poetry and morality. What parades itself as the literary-aesthetic ideology of our own age will receive attention later on in this lecture.

These various perspectives on literature may look like self-serving proclamations, coming as they do, from the literary practitioners themselves. But there is so much in literature which justifies their claims, so much force in the magic of the written word which roots the present in the past making sure we do not forget. Virtually all the personality types which populate the world and its complex terrain can be located in the works Shakespeare created almost four centuries ago. My first contact with Mark Twain was in 1962, in high school. Even at that tender age, my classmates and I were able to identify with Tom Sawyer's and Huckleberry Finn's journeys through the wilds of the Mississippi, we too being young like them, restless like them, inhabiting a part of the world that is also blessed with thick forests and large rivers, and above all, being sharers of the same sky and similar human impulses. Whitman, Thoreau, Langston Hughes, Margaret Walker, Neruda, Marquez, Raja Rao, Dostoievsky, Gorky, Lu Hsun, Soyinka, Achebe, Ngugi, Nadine Gordimer, Brathwaite, Walcott and many, many others have created, are creating, images and ideas which enrich humanity across the world. No matter what their places of origin, no matter what the period of composition of their works, a certain thread binds them to the bundle of our human experience; for literature, like the other arts, is not only trans-temporal, it is also trans-spatial—a fact which led the Soviet writer Yuri Bondarev to see true works of art as "the immense spiritual energy of a nation, its experience and memory".[3]

But our argument so far is guilty of a certain grapho-centricism, for we have argued as if all there is to literature is the written word. And this is far from true, because as the Yoruba say,

Omi tootoo	Water is supreme
Omi o	Oh water
Omi la te	For water is what we tread
Ka to te yanrin	Before we step on sand

Yes, the spoken word is the "water" of discourse which nurtured our venturing feet before the final encounter with the "sands" of written symbols. The folktale pre-dated the novel, the ballad, the scribbled sonnet; proverbs, aphorisms, idioms, and other gnomic sayings are the scriptless library of an oral culture; memory is their anchor, effortless recall the mark of their eloquent mastery. There are countless parts of the world where the culture of print is still making a slow entry. Here, in addition to the spoken word, the people's memory resides in the throbbing alphabet of the drum, and the learned execution of dance steps. The people are not only proud of their oral culture, they are more critical of the written lore. As the griot of the epic of Sundiata has observed about writing, "... this invention has killed the faculty of memory... for writing lacks the human voice". Our griot is, justifiably, suspicious of learning "congealed in books".[4]

Hitherto, we have argued as though every writer is concerned with human memory, as though every writer possesses the passion for creating memorable works. But my experience of the literature of our times—in both its creative and critical capacities—points in the other direction. For, this last quarter of the 20th century is witnessing a resurrection of the old formalism; but the new formalism lacks the theoretical vigor, methodological consistency, and analytical clarity of its old sire. Once again there is a vehement attempt to divorce content from form, banish substance from art, substitute tinsel surfaces for dark depths and strip literature of its affecting magic.

Not long ago, I received a letter inviting me to contribute to a poetry journal. Upon further perusal, I discovered that that letter was footnoted with "conditionalities": no inspirational poetry, no social poetry, no protest poetry, no message poetry, please! The editor's prescriptions nearly provoked me to parody: If I had the time for such trivialities, I would have sent him a poem on the slumber of my spoon, or a dry elegy (since he was so scared of juicy inspiration) on the assassination of a fingernail.

The prescription of this journal is just an instance of the insufferable inanity affecting the so-called modern art. Everywhere today, particularly in the industrial-developed parts of the world, there is a conscientious effort to run away from the kind of art that means, the type that affects. Literature, music, the cinema, and the visual arts are characterized by indulgent phantasmagoria, high-tec surreal scientificism, trivial abstractionism, a desperate attempt to say nothing. Science fiction, science film, space art, and so on have now shifted the horizontal relationships between human beings to vertical encounters between people and hair-raising aliens from other worlds. No thoughtful mind can fail to grasp the noisy escapism in all this, the modern man's attempt to take leave of himself, to jeopardize the commerce of human relationship, to snap the bond between himself and the Other.

Contemporary criticism panders to this kind of "hype" art, erecting all kinds of "post-modernist" modishness to lend it legitimacy. Feeling is estranged from art, reasoned optimism is jettisoned for inexplicable despair. And yet the critic "deconstructs" the work without looking at what Adrienne Rich calls the "world beyond the text".[5] For him, all that matters is the script and the delicate architectonics of its making. A post-mortem surgeon, he dissects a living work of art like a cold and friendless corpse.

Yet art matters, and as the authors of *American Memory* have succinctly and insightfully put it, "Words have consequences".[6] The world's memory is shaped by writers who labour stubbornly, incessantly, to humanize our consciousness, writers who have faith in the necessity of their mission, writers who, like the magnificent Walt Whitman, are ready to declare with eloquent assurance:

> I am not an earth nor an adjunct of an earth
> I am the mate and companion of people, all just as immortal
> And fathomless as myself,
> Every kind for itself and its own, for me mine male and female,

For me those that have been boys and that love women,
For me the man that is proud and feels how it stings
to be slighted,
For me the sweetheart and the old maid, for me
mothers
and mothers of mothers,
For me lips that have smiled, eyes that have shed tears,
For me children and the begetters of children?[7]

* Slightly modified version of the S.A. Yoder Memorial Lecture presented to the Convocation of Goshen College, Indiana, U.S.A., October 21, 1988.

Notes

1. D.T. Niane, *Sundiata: An Epic of Old Mali*, Transl. G.D. Pickett. Longman, 1973, p. 41.
2. Cheikh Hamidou Kane, *Ambiguous Adventure*. New York: Collier Books, 1971, p. 31.
3. Yuri Bondarev On Craftsmanship. Moscow: Raduga Publishers, 1984, p. 274. Sundiata, p. 41.
4. *Ambiguous Adventure*, p. 31.
5. Adrienne Rich, *Blood, Bread, and Poetry: Selected Prose*, 1979-1985. New York & London: W.W. Norton, 1986, p. 172.
6. *American Memory* (a Report on the Humanities in the Nation's Public Schools). National Endowment for the Humanities, 1988, p. 9.
7. Walt Whitman, 'Song for Myself', in *The Treasury of American Poetry*, ed. Nancy Sullivan. New York: Doubleday, 1978, p. 206.

*SQUARING UP TO AFRICA'S FUTURE:
A WRITER'S REFLECTIONS ON THE PREDICAMENTS OF A CONTINENT

In his letter inviting me to give today's lecture, Mr. Vincent Ogbuehi, president of the Nigerian Students' Union, enjoined me to "come to Norman to speak truth with power." Very exciting words. Very inspiring too. But I hope Mr. Ogbuehi knows the kind of risk he is asking me to take! My esteemed compatriot has made two flattering assumptions: 1) that I am in possession of the truth, 2) that I have power. I hereby confess to non-possession of these two attributes beyond the capacity of anyone seated here today. But I also confess to a reasonable capability for discerning the truth when I do or do not see it, and have learned, have been taught by the world, to recognise untruth whenever both of us meet on the alley of human experience, and to seek truth beyond the apocryphal affectations of its opposite. The power of truth inheres not in its ability to eliminate untruth (for no one can expect to kill their own shadow), but in its power to press on with its eternal struggle with untruth, making sure that tested virtue gains eventual victory over cowardly vice.

There is yet another risk which is both social and epistemological. In a world where truth is gasping in the iron grip of over-relativization, where one person's fact is another's fiction, and vice versa, where truth itself comes in different colours and a variety of plastic masks, isn't it true to say that one person's truth is another's heresy? For contemporary truth is not like the verity of old, immutable, constant, autolectic, and consistently empowering. It is invented, constructed, deconstructed in a baffling battery of textualities.

Africa, our continent, is a curious text in this array of figurations. Her truth has always been a victim of master-truths, invented or constructed beyond her borders by those whose calculated, self-serving fictions are often passed off as superior, unassailable fact of the African condition. Put another way, Africa's truth has always been at the mercy of the fiction of others. This is a process so pernicious that the African has abandoned the truth of the self for the fiction of the other.

This state of things need not continue. Hence the peculiar wording of my topic for this lecture: "Squaring up to Africa's Future..." My lexical choice is motivated by a nagging experiential imperative: the humiliations and abasements of the past (and present), the squandered hopes, aborted dreams, the several treacheries by those whom History once gave the chance of re-routing our destiny, the lethargy of our people, our snail-crawl in a world of supersonic celerity; in short, Africa's continuing weakness in a world dominated by the strong. These debacles should be seen, however, as cause for positive action, not excuse for disabling despondency. The subject of today's lecture, therefore, springs from an impulse that is both affirmative and interrogative. For the essence of the Black Heritage Month of which today's event constitutes a part is the need to constantly engage the past, examine the present, anticipate and pre-figure the future; the need to sharpen Memory and empower Vision, two attributes without which a people perish.

These sentiments, these questions, these truths were at the heart of my consciousness throughout the composition of Midlife, my latest volume of poems, a volume made up of strands of my own biography, and threads of the troubled annals of Africa, of the world. The first paragraph of the "Foreline" summarises my rather ambitious project:

> Midlife. Noontide in the diary of the sun. Dawn has raced quietly by, twilight peeps in from a compass of looming shadows. Past forty now, the riddling kola of life ripening, ripening in my mouth... Taller too, able to look the giant in the face, able to ask Africa a few sunny questions about her dormant dawn. Able to ask the world how many wasted nights really make a single day...[1]

The entire sixth movement of this volume is an engagement— sometimes affirmative, sometimes dubitative, sometimes consolatory, sometimes frustrating—with the perplexing configuration called Africa, "a continent so ancient and so infant", the "deciduous laughter of (her) winds", and the evergreen smile on her bruised lips. I keep asking why Africa is "Giving, all ways giving", taking little or nothing in return; and in the end,

> My question, Africa, is a sickle, seeking ripening laughters in your deepening sorrows[2]

This is a volume whose gestation began as soon as I turned forty. In 1947 when I beheld the light outside the womb in a lowly farmer's house in Ikere-Ekiti in the western part of Nigeria, the world was still clearing the debris of what some historians call the Second World War. Though Africans were conscripted into that war, and Africa's resources were committed to boosting the war effort of different colonial masters engaged in the campaign, it took (or is taking) several years to eliminate in Africa the vices and crimes over which the world engaged Hitler and his allies in bloody combat. I was ten years old when Ghana led other African countries in throwing off the colonial yoke, and thirteen in 1960 when my country Nigeria, and a number of other African nations, attained independence. I was already a university teacher in 1975 when Mozambique and Angola wrested their freedom from Portugal; and had just submitted Midlife for publication in 1990 when Namibia, at last, sang her freedom song.

There is thus a vital interpenetration between my life as a person and a writer, and the torturous odyssey of Africa, my continent. This is why after forty years on her bosom I began to ask how old Africa herself has been, how tall. For in my first two score years on earth, I have seen Africa's lamp of hope which burned so brightly, enthusiastically in the 60's and 70's, attenuate into a flicker in the 80's, almost snuffed out as humanity put its foot on the last ten rungs of the ladder of the 20th century. I have seen a puny, demonic clown crown himself emperor in a reckless ceremony that ate up a substantial portion of his country's resources; I have seen an aged king impose the world's second largest basilica on the baffled countryside of a sorely indebted country. I have seen fire-eating "revolutionaries" and "nationalists" soften into ice-cream-sucking presidents-for-life. I have seen freedom, human dignity shrink in Africa while tyrants who rule by what Wole Soyinka the Nobel Laureate has described as the divine right of the gun, define their bizarre power by the number of prisons and detention centers in their unfortunate domain. I have seen former food baskets turn into hunger deserts while a fifth of the continent's population eke out a precarious existence from begging bowls and hand-outs from international aid-givers. I have never ceased asking Africa how that cradle of humankind so haplessly became humankind's laughing stock.

The past opens before me like a book of luminous lines; I see the paths taken, the paths not taken, and the paths mistaken. I perceive the long shadows cast by Africa's predicament, the sour grapes of the past which have set our contemporary teeth on edge. I interrogate History in the dock of human experience, and History talks back in a running mix of eloquence and silence.

Of course, I am far from being the only African wrier concerned with probing the African predicament. This preoccupation is, indeed, the burden of African letters, its rallying clarion, its organising principle. From Olaudah Equiano to Soyinka, from Phyllis Wheatley to Ama Ata Aidoo; in the powerful fiction of Achebe, Armah, Ngugi wa Thiong'o, La Guma, Bessie Head, Nawal el Saadawi; in the forthright, insightful film and fiction of Sembene Ousmane; the poetry of Brutus, Awoonor, Clarke-Bekederemo, Kunene, Mnthali,

Mtshali; in the engaging drama of Soyinka, Penina Muhando, Rotimi, Osofisan, Hussein, Sowande, Dongala, Gebre Medhin, Tess Onwueme; in the polyphonic voices of Ekwensi, Sofola, Mapanje, Okai, Ofeimun, Angira, Ojaide, Omotoso, Iyayi, Chipasula, Ndebele, Hove, Abdilatif Laabi, Okri, Anyidoho.

These writers and several others have combined the excellence of art with the urgency of social relevance, posing new answers for old questions, new questions for old answers, denouncing the agents of Africa's backwardness without failing to point up the possibility of hope. In squaring up to Africa's monster, some of them have been bruised and bloodied, some have had to sacrifice their personal freedom, a recent painful example being Jack Mapanje, the poet and humanist who has been held incommunicado in his native Malawi since 1987.[3] The price for speaking up is high: the towncrier often has the hangman's noose very close to his or her throat; but the cost of silence would be even higher for Africa's future.

About two decades ago, Basil Davidson, one of the most perceptive and humane scholars of African history, wondered aloud in a small book titled Can Africa Survive? Davidson's alarm stemmed from the deep-felt anxiety of a genuinely committed Africanist whose knowledge of Africa's saga of plunder and impoverishment gave him little cause for optimism. A few months later, Emmanuel Obiechina, one of Africa's most erudite literary critics fired back a categorical, patriotic reply, 'Africa Shall Survive.' Between the nuanced, somewhat rhetorical question of Davidson and the clear, affirmative rejoinder of Obiechina lies the true tenor of the articulation of Africa's protean predicament.

Noteworthy is the significant recurrence of the word "survive" in both writings. The word connotes struggle, strife, travail, the confronting of overwhelming odds, and the sense of a chancy escape. It signifies a battle-weary, shell-shocked fighter crawling out of the debris and smokes of a brutal encounter, rather than a triumphant warrior with a stained sword or spear, resplendent in colorful garlands. For to "survive" is to exist, or to be lucky enough to exist; both words are qualitatively different from to live. Managing to keep head above water is surely not the same as swimming across a shark-infested ocean with bold and definite strokes that lead to a secure shore.

There are so many reasons why Africans and others genuinely interested in the African predicament should feel concerned. Africa is the most humiliated, most dehumanised continent in the world. Her history is a depressing tale of dispossession and impoverishment. This is a continent which contributed her most valuable assets—her sons and daughters—to the development and advancement of other places in the world. And even now she has nothing to show for the exploitation of her several natural resources: her gold, silver, diamond, copper, etc.; her cocoa, coffee, cashew, tea, etc. I have never stopped wondering how—and why—a continent can be so rich and yet so poor.

There are other more subtle but equally pernicious sides to this impoverishment. And here I am making a point which is hardly new but which needs being made all the same. Hand in hand with Africa's loss of human and natural resources went a drastic whittling down of her dignity. From the racist accounts of explorers engaged in voyages of "discovery", to those of squint-eyed anthropologists, to the ethnocentric fictions of Joyce Cary, Elspeth Huxley, Rider Haggard, Joseph Conrad and several others, the image of Africa that hits the eye is that of a jungle, zoo, cottage farm, or at best a wild orchard in the backyard of the world. Rudyard Kipling's "half-devil, half-child" representation of the African issues directly from a long tradition of racist arrogance. It is common knowledge now that Granville Sharpe and other abolitionists were asked to provide proof that the black person was indeed human, and therefore deserving of equal treatment with real human beings. The German philosopher Hegel completed this project of absence and negation (apologies to Henry Louis Gates) by denying Africa any claim to History, by excising a whole continent from the world's historical process. So you can see that Trevor Roper, the Regius Professor at Oxford, was not so original after all in his very learned pontification that the "dark continent" has no history.

We can understand the self-serving motive behind these "opinions". We may even be prepared to consign them to the blind spot in the curious eye of history; but how do we explain the "theories" of the genetic wizards of the 20th century, those prince merchants of the Intelligence Quotient (IQ) fetish, who have arranged humanity into a race hierarchy with the Black person far out at the bottom, a few insignificant rungs above the ape? Perhaps you want to say there is nothing new here. The authenticity of the black person has always suffered in the laboratory of pseudo-science.

All these negations, of course, have their social and psychological repercussions. Every black person in the world today, no matter his or her status, is victim of an oppressive racist heritage. As a person of colour you are considered, *a priori*, another grinning, eye-rolling negro with mush between his ears until you can prove that you too are capable of the Cartesian cogito. As a black person from Africa, you are regarded abroad as, inevitably, the victim of a continent-wide famine and plague from which you have been rescued by the mothering arms of Europe and America. Let me illustrate with a recent experience.

I was invited for poetry reading by one of the universities not far from here. After finishing my business with the adult section of the university community, I was asked to do a short reading at an elementary school close by, an invitation I very happily accepted. And I was not disappointed. My young hosts filled up the entire school gym, and they were a most appreciative, most inspiring audience. But just as I stepped out after the reading, a sharp, attractive girl ran up to me for an autograph.

"Thank you for your reading", she said, "I have never experienced a performance of that kind".

"Thank you too for being such a wonderful audience", I said back.

"But tell me, is it true you're from Africa?"

"Yes", I said.

"How then are you so big? I mean....you don't look thin like the Africans I see on tv".

I knew instantly the radix malorum. I knew American tv had come between me and my human dignity. But I nursed no anger. I sat my young friend down and told her that Africa is a large continent with hungry parts and parts that are not so hungry. We exchanged addresses. She promised to visit Nigeria someday when she is much older. And I promised her lots of pounded yam and palm wine....

Without any attempt at undue racial differentiation, I want to stress that only those who inhabit the black skin can know the haunting, harrowing specters in its beleaguered castle; the fact that as a black person you are consciously or unconsciously defensive from the cradle to the grave; the fact that you have to fight and struggle for the rights and dignity the other races have come to take for granted; the fact that you are engaged with a world which constantly others and marginalises your being and essence; the fact that you have to spend an entire life span just struggling to spell your name.

Africa is, of course, a human continent with all her virtues and vices, her beast and beauty. We have to tell ourselves and each other a few home truths. As my father used to say, when a chicken brings home a snake from the bush in the backyard, you do away with the snake first, then ask the chicken what frivolity drove it to the snake's territory. Today, according to Ali Mazrui, Africa has within its domain "thirty of the world's hungriest nations". Virtually every African country is heavily—and unaccountably—indebted; some have even gone completely bankrupt. We are going through a second slavery which is more vicious than the first: this time the chains are gold and silver; the masters are the trans-national finance conglomerates; the slave-sellers are the corrupt African political elite.

More children are out of school now than two decades ago; more people are perishing from avoidable diseases; fewer shelters are being built; fewer roads are being constructed. In conjunction with these problems, or, indeed, arising from them, the landscape is littered by tyrants, dictators, and sit-tight presidents incessantly doing violence to our social and political psyche. Those who vowed to rule have continued to mule their subjects; leaders have turned into dealers. The magnitude of political and economic corruption is so stunning that some rulers are richer than their entire countries.

All kinds of cause have been advanced for Africa's perennial underdevelopment. One of these causes is leadership. Indeed,

Africa's foremost novelist, Chinua Achebe, came to this conclusion when he said categorically that *The Trouble with Nigeria* is "simply and squarely" that of leadership.[4] There is also a submission, sometimes cynically made, that a country gets the kind of leadership it deserves. This may be true of an advanced, truly open democracy in which political choice is unhampered and enlightened. But to apply this axiom to the several countries of Africa and the so-called Third World is to rub salt in the bleeding wound of a people. Besides, the crucial question to ask is: why are patriotic, purposeful, honest, and visionary leaders in Africa always so short-lived? What or who is responsible for the murderous longevity of sit-tight despots and dictators with their corrupt, corrupting courtiers and depraved dynasties?

The problems facing Africa and, therefore, the future we have to square up to are protean and octopus-like. As I hinted before, some of the issues I have raised in this lecture are not so new; some are the same old ideas couched in new words. So let it be. For as our people say, *Ti ina ko ba tan laso, eje ko ki i kuro leekan* (As long as there are lice in the garment, there must be bloodstanis on the finger-nails). There is a lot to be done in giving Africa a new lease on life. Nothing can be achieved by papering over her cracks or by pretending (as is customary in sickening diplomatic circles) that the problems do not exist.

We, especially the youth, are not just the world; we are also the answer. But we cannot be the right answer until we have got ourselves to understand the Question (note the capital 'Q'). The Question explodes into a panoply of sub-questions: who are we? where are we? where did we come from? where are we heading? Answering these questions involves throwing off the yoke of History, turning that prison of our skin into a palace of hope, understanding Africa, denouncing her vices, nursing her virtues. Above all, it means believing in ourselves.

In concrete terms it means cultivating the spirit of hard work, frugality, resourcefulness. No people can ever develop without these. Our present state of social, cultural, and psychological confusion, our "Westernization without technical modernization" has led to the following disturbing, but brutally frank comments by Ali Mazrui:

Africa as a whole borrowed the wrong things from the West— even the wrong components of capitalism. We borrowed the profit motive but not the entrepreneurial spirit. We borrowed the acquisitive appetites of capitalism but not the creative risk-taking. We are at home with Western gadgets but are bewildered by Western workshops. We wear the wrist-watch but refuse to watch it for the culture of punctuality. We have learned to parade in display, but not to drill in discipline. The West's consumption patterns have arrived, but not necessarily the West's technique of production.[5]

One of my principal hosts here today, Olayinka Akande, sent me a moving poem in our inaugural correspondence. Titled "Laughing to Cry", it is an affectionate, nostalgic but questioning address to Africa: "When will I be able to return to my own America?... When can I go home again?" To these questions, my answer is: make it soon! For if we do not join hands in rescuing Africa, no one will do it for us. If Africa does not develop because of us, it will now develop in spite of us. We need to keep the lamp of hope burning, for as I once said in one of my early poems:

Our dream will not wither
In the cradle of night
We shall not die
In our sleep

It is only we that can wipe the tears from the face of our embattled continent. And I have infinite faith in our ability to do it. We can make Africa a strong community of peoples where social justice is empowered by those humanistic values for which our part of the world is widely known.

I was invited here to "speak truth with power". I know I have spoken with some measure of power. I can only hope that in doing so I have also spoken a modicum of Truth.

---

*   Black Heritage Month Lecture, The University of Oklahoma at Norman, February 25, 1991.

Notes

1. Niyi Osundare, *Midlife*. Ibadan: Heinemann Educational Books, 1993, p. ix.
2. Midlife, p. 98.
3. Jack Mapanje has since been released.
4. Chinua Achebe, *The Trouble With Nigeria*. Enugu: Fourth Dimension Publishers, 1983, p. 1.
5. Ali Mazrui, *Cultural Forces in World Politics*. Portsmouth: Heinemann Educational Books; London: James Currey Ltd., 1990, p. 5.

OF PRIZES AND MESSIAHS

The news of Ben Okri's Booker Prize could not have come at a more auspicious time. Arriving so close on the heels of the Clarence Thomas - Anita Hill sexual harassment fiasco, it brought a most welcome balm to our wounded psyche by confirming—for all who cared to listen—the need to shift attention from the myth between the Black person's thighs to the repressed genius between his/her ears.

And for Okri as a person and a writer, the award is an invaluable oasis on a long and famished road, a most-needed—and most deserved—reward for an author's single-minded, rigorous, and almost demonic dedication to the promise of the pen. Of course, I have always had problems with the melodramatic, sometimes scatological figurations in aspects of Okri's narrative, especially their pessimistic evisceration of the Nigerian landscape; but I am also forcibly struck by Okri's irrepressibly humane impulse, his angry, even pugnacious consciousness—at war with evil, at war with those who make the world too large or too small. No one can miss the tough intellectual energy in an Okri fiction, his almost frantic devotion to art.

So, glad I was when news came of Okri's triumph. But I was also scared that soon, very soon, focus would shift from the novel that won the award to a specious archaeology of African writing. I knew literary statisticians would go to work, with a running spectacle of firsts: 'the first Nigerian novelist to...,' 'the first African novel to...,' 'the first African to...,' etc. I knew literary speculators would go to town with brave projections of the inestimable 'focus' the prize would confer on African literature, the much-needed 'attention' it would endow African writing with, the abundant 'recognition' that African letters would reap from it....

My fears emanated from a personal experience. Upon co-winning the Commonwealth Poetry Prize in 1986, I was flattered, then infuriated by commentators who kept congratulating me on putting Nigerian, nay African literature, 'on the map'. Remember this was the year the inimitable Wole Soyinka captured the father of all literary prizes, the Nobel, a feat which many thought would convert, finally, the unknown beast called African literature into a venerable beauty toasted at cocktail parties from Dodan Barracks to Buckingham Palace. Now five full years later, another African has won a prestigious prize and the same 'focus-recognition-map' drums are loud in the streets.

The questions that keep coming to my mind are: whose 'recognition'? Which cartographer drew this 'map' in a way that Africa has to struggle for a place on it? When did literary prizes become an entire continent's entry condition to the artistic patrimony of the world?

In a curious but logical way, the focus-attention-recognition shibboleth is offspring of a deep-seated exofugal anxiety that is itself an offshoot of the center-margin dichotomy that characterises Africa's relationship with the outside world. By the logic of this anxiety, Europe and the United States form the center of the world; Africa and other 'Third World' countries are consigned to the margin. And, naturally, the margin is that proverbial abode of the wretched of the earth, the roost of chaotic silence where nothing has a life of its own, by its own, without an enabling nod from outside. On the other hand, the center occupied as of right by powerful nations, is a model held up to the world, a place where everything happens, confirmer of value, even credibility, the ultimate arbiter of literary and aesthetic taste.

The pull in all directions, all respects, is therefore towards the centre. And this situation has generated an intriguing irony: to be fully appreciated at home, many African writers have to seek 'recognition' abroad. If a foreign critic decides that an African writer is good or bad, who is the home-grown critic to say it is otherwise? Who will hear his/her voice? The margin is the center of silence. It swallows up the voice, complete with its echoes. The town crier's cadence is muted in dreary mists. Only ventriloquists of foreign gods are left in the streets.

The center calls the shots, moderates the debate (which very often sidles from dialogue to monologue), apportions speaking (and hearing) rights, dictates voice modulation, determines who is to be heard or hushed. The center is where 'best-sellers' are born and bred. Which is why not a few writers would do anything, anything, to get reviewed—or simply mentioned—in *The Times* either of London or New York, but hardly of New Delhi or Lagos. As the Nigerian writer Kole Omotoso once remarked, to be worth real attention at home today, the African writer must have imported 'recognition' from abroad. Only few sympathetic newspapers would risk wasting their increasingly scarce resources on what in Nigeria is derisively called a 'local champion.'

African universities, those citadels of marginal silence, have done everything to advance this exogenous pathology. Until recently, books and articles 'published abroad' weighed heavier in the consideration for promotion. It was (is) more rewarding, more civilised, to do a study of Ben Jonson than of Wole Soyinka; to explicate the terminal 'e' in pre-Chaucerian English than carry out analysis of Sierra Leonean *krio* or Nigerian pidgin. Just as our economists keep telling us to produce what can be sold in Europe, what can bring in the sorely needed foreign exchange, even at the expense of domestic wealth and subsistence, our writers are being urged to put their pen where their fame is, to write themselves out of marginal obscurity.

In a strange way, the margin fosters its own narcissism, its own hysterical craving for an image, not in its own mirror (the margin does not have its own mirror), but in that of the center. The projection therein is usually not that of the self, but of the self as defined and determined by the other. And the center that manufactures all these mirrors recognises its own replications, its own marginal copies. The gods can spot their own voice even in the darkest recesses of the ventriloquist's throat.

At work in the 'recognition' anxiety is a curious complementary consciousness. On the one hand is a mindset of the center that grants high-priced recognition to those African works which conform to and reinforce that traditional Euro-American opinion about Africa. In this regard, some Western critics actually believe that their attention, their patronage, is enough to win instant 'recognition' for an African work. And, what's more, that it is their inalienable right to bestow such recognition.

This attitude is enhanced and perpetuated by the belief of the margin that no work can be deemed accomplished until it has been judged so by the center. After all, all the canons, whether in creative writing or literary theory, have *always* originated from centers outside Africa. And when these canons boom, the margin scurries about like chickens, picking up fall-outs, basking in the hand-me-down vibrations of expiring idioms. Which is why in the prevailing discourse of the world today, the center inaugurates the voice, the margin scrambles for the echoes.

This unequal discourse is heir to nonliterary antecedents. Shake out the drawers of history, and you will discover that Africa has never played the name-giver in international affairs; on the contrary, she has always been the named. The Niger didn't exist until Mungo Park 'discovered' it; Kinshasa was not there until it acquired the name of Belgium's Leopold; that magnificent lake between Kenya, Uganda, and Tanzania was a mute, indeterminate body of water until it was 'discovered' by Speke, 'explored' by Stanley, then named for Queen Victoria. Go through the length and breadth of this wonderful world, you will find no continent that has surrendered so much to foreign Adams.

But why will outsiders not be in a position to judge *for* us on what is good or bad about our literature? Why should we not die to gain their attention, win their recognition? Hasn't William

Blake, that fecundly revolutionary English poet, warned that those who do not/cannot create their own system must be prepared to be enslaved by the system of others? Africa is not only a continent in the margin, but by every indication she appears so inexorably, so fatally pleased to be there.

Just consider this: apart from the omnibus Noma Award which has come to be through the generosity and vision of a Japanese publisher, there is no single continental literary prize of substantial worth in Africa. This crucial lack must be laid at the door of a monster other than our perennial poverty. Or how does one plead poverty in this regard in a continent where one country sometimes squanders several million dollars on hosting a continental conference, a continent where a sit-tight dictator is so scandalously rich that he has been described as a "walking bank account in leopard skin hat"? No, Africa's failure to institute her own literary prizes is due to monumental lack of vision by African rulers, their proverbial hostility to images and ideas of beauty, their rank philistinism, their eternal satisfaction at being 'movers and shakers' of the margin. No, the African strongman would rather build a prison for the writer than establish a prize for his/her artistic accomplishment.

But let us go back to our argument about foreign 'recognition' and the exogenous determination of the value of African literature and art. There are many reasons why we should not blame Africans who thank their prize-winning compatriots for bringing 'recognition' to the continent. Africa has remained for many centuries a victim of negation and absence. The accomplished writer from Africa is, therefore, regarded not just as a voice, but also as an antidote, a veritable medal to be waved in the face of a humiliating and relentlessly cynical world, a proof that we too have not come to the gathering of the world with empty hands. The book was a powerful instrument in the oppression and exploitation of the African; the book is also seen by many Africans today as a weapon of liberation. So whether they accept that mantle or not, modern African writers are regarded as warriors, the literary messiahs of a silenced and much-abused tribe.

To be sure, foreign prizes and their attendant recognition have played a valuable diplomatic role in the lives and struggles of

African literary ambassadors. But for pressures and outcry consequent upon their recognition abroad, Soyinka, Ngugi, Nawal el Saadawi, Abdilatif Laâbi, Micere Mugo, Jack Mapanje, and many others would probably not have come out alive from the dungeons of African strongmen. The 1988 Commonwealth Fiction Prize came as an invigorating poetic justice to Festus Iyayi, a fine Nigerian novelist and leader of Nigeria's Academic Staff Union of Universities (ASUU), who flew to London for the prize only a few days after emerging from a prolonged and gruesome detention without charge, without trial.

So this essay is by no means another vulgar attack on foreign prizes and awards. It has nothing against recognition provided it is healthy, genuine, and unpatronizing. The thrust of its argument is that there is something essentially universal about the genius of human creativity, no matter what is provenance. No part of the world has a right to lay a monopolistic claim to that genius, and proceed to lay out parameters and yardsticks for the artistic estate of other places. The world is a wide, miraculous *mbari* to which every people bring their own creation. Let no one play master in that gathering. Let no one accept to play servant. Let no canons terrorise talents with arrogant booming.

Above all, Africa needs to discover her own name without making other continents anonymous; she needs to find her own center without marginalising other parts of the world.

AFRICAN LITERATURE AND THE CRISIS OF POST-STRUCTURALIST THEORISING

Interrogating the Interrogators

Let me begin by confessing to a nagging unease about the 'post-ness' tagged on to contemporary theorising in general: post-structural, post-modernist, post-colonial, post-Marxist, post-industrial, etc. There is also talk about the 'posthumanist' era, though we hope in all earnestness that the 'post-human' society will never arrive! This innocuous-looking prefix, 'post', kicks up temporal, spatial, even epistemological problems, operates most times on a set of fallacies which seduce us into a false consciousness that human thoughts, ideas, actions, experiences, and the significant events they generate are arrangeable in a linear, x-before - y - y - after - x framework, very much like a series of temporal scenarios in an overdeterministic succession.

Implicit in this linear arrangement is a suggestion of misleading chronology, a temporo-ideational fiction which constructs progression as a process in which ideas are used and discarded, then superseded and supplanted by new ones. This method hardly looks back except for self-justification and self authentication1, it is so full of contemporaneist bravado about the relative (at times absolute) superiority of its own perceptual ideology, theoretical re-categorization and analytical methodology.

However, the prefix 'post' raises issues of a fundamental philosophical nature. When used with a temporal signifier, it acquires a clearer, more orginary power than when yoked up with the ideational. Compare 'post-1945' and 'post structuralist'. While it is possible to point to January 1946 as the specific, immediate commencement of 'post 1945', we would be hard put to it to tell specifically when 'post-structuralism' began—the time and place it was born, its progenitors, its birth-weight, the attending midwives, etc. This is why, despite the several claimants to its orginary authorship, we still find it difficult to say in unmistakable terms who the 'founders' of post-structuralism were or are. There is an inevitable fuzziness, even indeterminacy, about these things which theories of the 'post-' variety are often too hasty to admit.

It is an irony that a theoretical theology such as poststructuralism whose principal tenet is the deconstruction of dichotomy should have its own temple erected on a similar binarism: structuralism versus post-structuralism, modernism versus post-modernism, etc. For one of the abiding concerns of the New Historicism is the reconstruction of our view of history not as a progressional, evolutionary inevitability, but as a multidirectional network of ruptured continuities in which cause may be effect, effect cause, a complex, supratemporal artifact in which the present derives its force from the unpastness of the past.

Post-structuralist practice understands this temporal and ideational fluidity, even if its theory appears to negate it. More than any other literary theory in recent times, post-structuralism derives a great number of its paradigms from the 'unpastness of the past'. In a rarely eclectic case of archaeology and necromancy, deconstructionists have exhumed the sagacious bones of Plato, Nietzsche, Schlegel, Hegel, Schopenhauer, Heidegger, Marx, Sartre, Bakhtin, etc. For critical and analytical terminologies (and methods) they have dug deep into the catacombs of classical and medieval rhetoric for such terms as: tropes, topos, metaphor, metonymy, hypostasis, aporia, polysemy, etc., which they have dusted up and sent on 'new' post-structuralist errands.

There is thus a significant 'bending over backwards' in post-structuralism, a rummage through the jungle of primeval epochs. How really self-assuredly new, then, are these terminologies, these methods, even in their new significations and functions, when their very origination interrogates the 'post-ness' of their 'structuralism'? Most times the old-new wine of post-structuralist analytical idioms feel quite ill at ease in the old wine-skin of their theory. Contemporary literary discourse is thus clogged with mongrel jargon, cultic, very professionalized, trapped in hermetic closures. The newer things appear to be, the older they really are.

How "post-colonial" is post-colonial discourse?
The world is shaped—and frequently determined—by the words we use for expressing it. In naming the world we also name ourselves, evoking a recognizable, tangible construct of that panoply of realities which constitute what we call the human experience. Names serve as the door to the house of experience, a guide to hidden meanings in the shadowy nooks of time and place. Names tell stories, liberate or imprison; they may also serve as self-fulfilling prophecies. Names commit; which is why the Yoruba say that it is only mad people who do not mind what names they are called, or who refuse to see the difference between the names they choose to bear and the ones the world prefers to call them by. The negative 'politics of representation' so famous in contemporary literary discourse is very much the product of misapprehension as it is of mis-naming and mis-verbalization. There are times people do not need to call a dog a bad name to hang it. The bad name does the hanging itself.

Conscious of the politics of naming, many African writers have expressed profound apprehension about the term 'post-colonial' as applied to the African situation in general and African writing in particular. For instance, speaking at a Commonwealth conference in London in 1991, Ama Ata Aidoo, playwright and novelist, challenged her audience in these words: "Ask any village woman how post-colonial her life is". Colonialism, she added, "has not been 'posted' anywhere at all."[2] Most appropriately, the paper from which these words emerged was titled "Collective Amnesia and the Role of the African Writer".

First let us collectively remember to ask a few questions: whose invention or re-invention is the term 'post-colonial'? Who was the first to apply it to the writings of Africa and other parts of the developing world? Since when has it become fashionable, theoretically and critically correct, to refer to these parts of the world by this term? What social and cultural constructions are thrust up by this concept? How are we committed by this term having so profoundly naturalized its meaning without pausing to think about its implications? To re-echo our former trope, this terminology names us, but do we know its own name and the origin and giver of that name?

It is pertinent to ask these questions, for the term 'post-colonial' is not just another literary-critical construct to be used with the same terminological certitude and blissful complacency with which we employ its counterparts such as 'post-structural', 'post-modernist', etc. More than other terminologies of the 'post-' variety, 'post-colonial' is a highly sensitive historical, and geographical term which calls into significant attention a whole epoch in the relationship between the West and the developing world, an epoch which played a vital role in the institutionalization and strengthening of the metropole-periphery, center-margin dichotomy. We are talking about a term which brings memories of gunboats and mortars, conquests and dominations, a term whose accent is blood-stained. We are talking about a term whose 'name' and meaning are fraught with the burdens of history and the anxieties of contemporary reality.

The first of these burdens concerns the politics of the genealogy of the term 'post-colonial'. Like many other phrases and concepts which define the African reality, this terminology owes its origination to foreign Adams. It is yet another instance of a 'name' invented for the African experience from outside, a 'name' which finds little or no acceptance among its African objects. It is undoubtedly this conflict between the African reality and the exogeneist determination and representation of it that led Firinne N. Chreachain to this conclusion about the Commonwealth conference mentioned earlier on in this essay: "It is obvious to anyone familiar with British Africanist circles that a vast gulf exists between critical perspectives within Africa and those prevalent among British Africanists."[3] (For 'British" substitute 'Western').

Chreachain's views here possess a thrust similar to that of Biodun Jeyifo in his critique of the "exclusively and prescriptively Western monument of High Theory." Jeyifo observes further:

> the contemporary understanding of theory not only renders it an exclusively Western phenomenon of a very specialized activity, but also implicitly (and explicitly) inscribes the view that theory does not exist, cannot exist outside of this High Canonical Western orbit.[4]

This apprehension about the imperialism of theory is by no means an exclusively African concern. In an interview with Gayatri Spivak in New Delhi, Rashmi Bhatnager, Lola Chatterjee and Rajeshwari Sunder Rajan took their learned guest to task on the use of 'First World elite theory' for the literatures of the 'colonies':

> Now there is a certain uneasiness here about the ideological contamination of theory by the specific historical origins which produce it and therefore about the implications of employing it in our own context. Would you defend the post-colonial intellectual dependence upon Western models as historical necessity?[5]

It is instructive to note that Spivak's short, cryptic, and evasive answer to this very important question indeed ends up in another question counter-posed to her interviewers: "What is an indigenous theory?"

For ideological and intellectual reasons, it must be stressed here that what is really at issue in this argument is not simply the provenance of theories, but the ease and complacency with which Western theories have taken over the global literary and intellectual arena, the way they inscribe themselves as though the other parts of the world were a *tabula rasa*. There is something ethnocentric about this 'universalism', an attitude and behavior which constitute the world's literary discourse into a monumental Western monologue. In several ways, this totalises literary experience and the way people relate to it. So rigidly located in one place, how can we see the Great Mask of the world from different angles?

The second problem with the term 'post-colonial' is its denotative and descriptive inadequacy. What are the semantic and sociosemiotic designations of this compounded word: beyond- colonial; past-colonial; after-colonial; free-from-colonial; anti-colonial, or simply not-colonial? In other words, is 'post-colonial' a qualitative tag or a mere temporal phase maker?

Bill Ashcroft, Gareth Griffiths, and Helen Tiffin (1989) wrestle bravely with the monster sprung up by this term when they declare in *The Empire Writes Back*, a very valuable even if controversial book:

> We use the term 'post-colonial' to cover all the cultures affected by the imperial process from the moment of colonization to the present day.[6]

This declaration gives the prefix morpheme 'post' a new and baffling meaning. At work here is an aberrant, one-catch-all metonymy in which the part is too small for the whole it is used to represent. The logic of this definition puts works as far apart as *When Love Whispers* (1947), *The Palmwine Drinkard* (1952), *Fragments* (1969), and *I Will Marry When I Want* (1982) in the same 'post-colonial' bag. There is no doubt that this container is also large enough to swallow the works of D. O. Fagunwa, or the poetry of Shabaan Robert!

Further down the page, attention shifts from 'culture' to place, and the authors disclose the enormous assortedness of the fishes in the post-colonial net: Africa, Australia, Bangladesh, Canada, the Caribbean, India, Malaysia, Malta, New Zealand, Pakistan, Singapore, South Pacific, Sri Lanka—and the U.S.A.! Needless to say, what we have here is an unconscionably mixed bag whose constitutive items are so gross and so general that very little room is left for the crucial specificities of individual parts. And what's more, to so liberally apply the 'post-colonial' label to places such as Africa and Australia, the Caribbean and Canada—places whose colonial pasts are so fundamentally different—is tantamount to mocking the real wounds of the colonial infliction where they are deepest and most enduring. We certainly need to distinguish formal and superficial coloniality in places like Canada, Australia and New Zealand from the systematic, exploitative—and, above all, racist - coloniality in the rest of the countries in the list.

Colonialism is a complex, protean monster with various levels, degrees, and complexions. Its intricate mutations defy a simple, short-hand name, its continuities make a mockery of a totalising, comprehensive nomenclature. Thus, Ashcroft et al.'s submissions that "The idea of 'post-colonial' literary theory emerges from the inability of European theory to deal adequately with the complexities and varied cultural provenance of post-colonial writing,"[7] sounds ironical in the face of the inadequacy of their own emergent 'ideal' itself.

And besides, who needs this adumbrative tag with its own 'false notions of the universal'? Wasn't this name invented by Western Theory as a convenient nomenclatural handle on their epistemic spheres of influence? To reiterate our earlier point, the tag 'post-colonial' is more useful for those who invented it than it is for those who are supposed to wear it, its passive signifieds. It rings truer for those who have 'posted' colonialism in posh conference halls and arcane seminar rooms conveniently far from the real battleground of colonial encounter.

And this explains the problem of misrecognition and the resultant misrepresentation plaguing the term 'post-colonial'. Whether used ideationally or temporally, the term lures us into a false sense of security, a seeming pastness of a past that is still painfully present. It is common knowledge (no longer restricted to social scientists, especially of the political economics persuasion) that to apply the term 'post-colonial' to the real situation in Africa today is to be plainly naive or majestically futuristic, no matter what the degree of metaphoric extension we are prepared to grant that term. We are talking about a continent with very little control over its economy and politics, whose intra-continental interactions are still dominated by the same old colonial languages—a continent so heavily indebted to the finance houses of the advanced industrialized world, that many of its governments are virtually under foreign receiverships. How can we talk so gliby, so confidently about the 'post-coloniality' of a place so neo-colonial? Shouldn't we distinguish 'flag post-coloniality' from its genuine, purposive namesake? We need a new dictionary of contemporary literary terms.

The term 'post-colonial' is thus more loaded, more polysemic, more positional than its inventors and users are readily aware of. It even carries an (unintended) taint. The word 'post-colonial' endows its principal morpheme 'colonial' with an orginary privilege. 'Colonial' carries the voice of the beginning; it is the moving force, the significant point of departure. African literature, oral or written, in whatever language and style, is presented as having no identity, no name except in reference to it. However, history frequently intervenes with its intriguing fluidity. Consider the example of Ayi Kwei Armah's *Two Thousand Seasons* written in the 'post-colonial' period, but whose content and politics are so aggressively pre-colonial; or Achebe's *Things Fall Apart*, written in the colonial period, but whose narrative thrust straddles both pre-colonial and colonial epochs. What name, relative to 'colonial' shall we call those epics which thrived in many parts of Africa when history was once-upon-a-time and the white man had not made his momentous entry? What makes a work 'post-colonial': the time and place of its author or its own intrisic subject?

Lastly, the phatic import of that term. How does it sound, how does it feel to be called a 'post-colonial' writer? Should Ngugi wa Thiong'o, Achebe, Aidoo, etc. feel happy for having attained the 'post-colonial' status? When you meet me in the corridors tomorrow would you congratulate me on my 'post-colonial' poetry? Is there anything worth talking about outside 'coloniality'? In brief, is there life besides 'coloniality'?

Undeconstructed Silences
All theories leak. Old assumptions give way to new ones. Preexisting platitudes get spruced up in new raiment, and what used to be called 'six' receives a brave new baptism of 'half-dozen'. Post-structuralism in its various mutations and manifestations is, no doubt, a grand ambitious project. Its grounding in history, philosophy, and linguistics certainly gave it a rigorous, even radical head-start. Its interrogative methods

have provoked answers from shadowy silences, or gingered those answers into further questions.

But like Oedipus, post-structuralism's swollen foot emanated from its origins. As an "exclusively and prescriptively Western"[8] theory, post-structuralism has erected the West into a monumental metonym for the world, another instance of that part which considers itself larger than the whole. Because Africa (and the rest of the developing world) is absent or absenced from the post-structuralist Master Theory, most of its theoretical and conceptual projects have proved grossly inadequate in the analysis and apprehension of issues and developments outside the Western orbit. Literary space is inundated by a plethora of 'new' terminologies, methods and discursive practices, but hardly are these matched by a new consciousness about the world outside Europe and the United States, by a new grasp of the social, political, economic and cultural specificities of those parts of the universe pushed to the fringe.

In no aspect is this exclusivist ideology more palpable than the dialect of the celebrated practitioners of contemporary theorising, their preoccupation with Western topoi and exempla, their cultivation of impenetrable jargon, their demonstration of utter lack of awareness about places and peoples outside their own locales. In fact, many aspects of post-structuralist theorising have made the humanization of discourse impossible, as a result of their fetishization of the text and its theory. The over-abstract, reified processes of contemporary theorising have hitherto not shown any efficient medium of recognizing, analysing and representing the urgent concrete specificities of the developing world. Old prejudices, myths, fallacies, and misconceptions have not been deconstructed; on the contrary, they have been reconstructed into faddish frameworks couched in new-fangled lingo. The interrogative power of contemporary theories has been severely selective.

Let us illustrate some of the points above by examining a new book on *Conrad: Heart of Darkness: Case Study in Contemporary Criticism.*[9] It must be said to the credit of this book that it provides a potentially solid pedagogical tool for the study of Conrad's most famous book. It is compact, well-researched, informative, a long-overdue attempt at bridging the gap between post-structuralist theorising and post-structuralist literary analysis. And it takes Conrad through the diversity of contemporary projects: a chapter each on Psychoanalytic Criticism; Reader-response Criticism; Feminist Criticism, Deconstruction; and the New Historicism.

I grabbed this book with effusive enthusiasm, eager to see Conrad's archetypal silence and ambivalences unravelled, the gaps in the tale filled in, the old parable interrogated with a revolutionary critical weapon in this last quarter of the 20th century. I was anxious to see which theoretical practice would be able to engage the story, enter the text, initiate a humane dialogue with Conrad, ask him why there are no African human beings in a 'yarn' whose setting is Africa. I was expecting a post-structuralist open surgery on Conrad's Heart of Darkness, but what I got is a complex series of evasions, open-eyed blindness, wilful forgetfulness, or simply, an intellectual and racial connivance with the European novelist.

Instead of a set of new, vigorous perspectives, what hit my eye were the same old critical shibboleths in tinsel post-structuralist phraseology: the Chinese box narrative structure; the dangerously thin divide between civilization (Europe) and barbarism (Africa); the ordeal of the civilized European mind when thrown into the heart of African darkness, and one or two suppressed murmurs about Conrad's view of imperialism. In none of these chapters is Conrad's systematic and pervasive dehumanization of Africans discussed, talk less of interrogated. Our critics simply join Conrad in a 'post-structuralist', 'post-colonialist' voyage down the Congo, they too being 'wanderers on a prehistoric earth' (H.O.D. p. 50) surrounded by 'black shadows (H.O.D. p. 3), 'black bones' (H.O.D. p. 31), cannibals splashing around and pushing (H.O.D. p. 49), appalled by the 'smelly mud' (H.O.D. p. 35) of the Congo - several miles, several centuries away from 'the tranquil dignity (H.O.D. p. 18) of the Thames. To them , too, Africa is nothing more than a "wild and passionate uproar" (H.O.D. p. 51)[10]

And yet, one of the most significant chapters in this book is on a 'reader-response' approach to The Heart of Darkness. Now, reader-response criticism operates through an empowerment of the reader, making her/him "an active, necessary, and often self-conscious participant in the making of a text's meaning".[11] Meaning becomes an event through which the reader comes to a deeper, fuller understanding of art and the persons and places it constructs or represents. The reader, too, is expected to live through the text, probe its absences, fill in its gaps. The act of reading thus becomes an art in itself, a conscious, dynamic process of unraveling. This process functions through collaboration or confrontation with the text and its orginary spirit.

It goes without saying that this chapter has opted for collaboration with Conrad, and his vision, or rather, with the western reader of Conrad and her/his vision. Or how could Adena Rosmarin have arrived at this "reading" of Conrad's color code:

> While it is true that dark men in this tale tend to behave in ways more moral and more civilized than do white men, virtually every critic notes, for example, that the near-starving cannibals on board keep their hungry eyes off their masters -darkness remains the place and mode of Marlo's terminal struggle with Kurtz.[12]

So much then for noble savages and benevolent cannibals and their missionary restraint! Rejoice, oh black anthropophagi! You are "more moral and more civilized" than white men in Africa. And you have the magnanimity of Conrad and the naivety of his critic to thank for this! And for this piece of unmatchable wisdom Rosmarin has the authority of "virtually every critic"[13] as source of ready appeal. Need we ask who such critics are, and what their intellectual and racial identity is?

On page 156 of this book, Rosmarin asks a crucial question: "What is the experience of reading *Heart of Darkness* like?" How I wish she had included the African in her group of respondents. But as is customary in most Western discourse on Heart of Darkness, the African is conspicuous by her/his very absence. Afterall, in Conrad's tale, it is the forests, the shrubs, the river which possess the active, transitive impulse; not the Africans who, in any way, are nothing more than a swarm of "naked breasts, arms, legs, and glaring eyes."[14] The African response can only matter if you agree that she/he is a human being in the first place. But if, like Conrad, you believe she/he is not, why should you waste precious time seeking the response of a savage beast?

Rosmarin's reader-response criticism of *Heart of Darkness* is a clear demonstration of the fundamental ethnocentrism of aspects of post-structuralist theorising, its several blindnesses, and pitfalls; and, in particular, of the new metaphysics of readerly power and authority. For the questions which are left perpetually unanswered include: Who is the reader? What kind of pre-text - social, cultural, ideological, epistemic, etc. - is she/he importing into the text? What are the reader's primal, unconscious, or subconscious conspiracies with the text? Is or isn't the text really what the reader means it to mean?

The chapter on *The New Historicism* and *Heart of Darkness* begins with a cautions, dubitative concession (the only such concession in the whole book): "It (H.O.D.) tells us little, perhaps, about Congolese peoples" (my emphasis).[15] But earlier on in the paragraph Ross Murfin has hit the reader with this magisterial 'new historicist' proclamation:

> A work of art, it (H.O.D.) is at the same time a kind of historical document. It undoubtedly presents as accurate a picture of a colonized Africa as many other supposedly non-fictional accounts written during the same period.[16]

By the impeccable logic of this assertion, Conrad's jaundiced fiction is Africa's historical fact, a European novel 'about' Africa becomes an 'accurate' chronicle of Africa by some other name. But there is some method in the madness of the above proclamation: the 'non-fictional accounts' mentioned as parallel text here are, indeed, most likely to contain the same 'history', being invariably the accounts of colonial functionaries, European missionaries, or various 'discoverers' and 'explorers' of the African 'darkness'. But some information about modern African historiography would have instructed Murfin on the kind of 'history' in such accounts. However, this is not the place to ask how much or what kind of African history our author knows. We can only wonder how seriously to take those critics who embark upon a 'new historicist' analysis without a thorough and comprehensive apprehension of the text and its context; critics who practice 'historicism' without history.

In fairness to Brook Thomas,[17] his new historicist analysis is the one that shows the most prominent awareness of the African in Heart of Darkness. Unfortunately this awareness only comes in brief, pale flickers, the analytical channel having got thoroughly clogged by mountains of received critical baggage.

For instance, Thomas follows in the old beaten path. Conrad remains for him the chronicler of human experience.[18] Africans, even of the late 19th century, "exist in a state prior to history,"[19] a journey to Africa is both a physical and temporal journey into darkness; African savagery is the context in which European civilization finds its truth; Africa remains the abode of the unconscious, contrasting sharply with Europe's triumphant rationality.

Most times Thomas's 'interrogative' reading leads to further perversity. Like Rosmarin (mentioned earlier on), he too awards Africans who accompany Marlow up the river a medal for restraint for not "killing and eating the whites,"[20] despite their lingering starvation. Even more intriguing is Thomas's reading of the following passage which is Conrad's clearest summative testament to the African's sub-humanity:

> The earth seemed unearthly. We are accustomed to look upon the shackled form of a conquered monster but there—there you could look at a thing monstrous and free. It was unearthly, and the men were—no, they were not inhuman. Well, you know, that was the worst of it - this suspicion of their not being inhuman...[21]

Note here the complex dubitabilities, the stalking, stammering syntax of a mind which puts the African's claim to humanity to a monologic European debate. Note the tortuous indirectness which finds expression in the choice of double negatives: "their not being inhuman." The word 'human' occurs twice in this passage, undermined each time by the negative prefix 'in-.' In the final analysis, the African's humanity is a mere 'thought', a 'suspicion', her/his relationship to the world dims into a 'remote kinship' from "the night of first ages." Conrad's Africans "howled and leaped, and spun, and made horrid faces;" engaged in a "wild and passionate uproar;" they were "ugly." In spite of these and several other implicit and explicit textual signals so prevalent in the novel, Thomas comes up with the conclusion that Conrad's narrative 'disrupts' commonplace racial prejudices. He seems to have been misled by the jejune 'Chinese box' narrative trickery which puts those rabidly racist words and thoughts in the mouth of a distant narrator while granting Conrad their creator an absolute indemnity.

Even so, Thomas reinforces rather than deconstructs the ontological binarism which confirms Conrad's studied Manichaeism:

the West	vs.	Africa
Future	vs.	Prehistory
European civilization	vs.	African savagery
Rational	vs.	Unconscious
Language	vs.	Silence
Light	vs.	Darkness
European Self	vs.	African Other

The last pair in the series is particularly important here. For although Thomas makes some attempt at critiquing the 'Eurocentric perspective which constructs itself into a Self that constantly distances 'the Other,' he himself demonstrates a Eurocentric inability to recognize that 'Other,' to apprehend her/his misrepresentation. This is partly so because, like Conrad and his critics, Thomas neither knows nor understands the African 'Other,' and therefore cannot sympathise with her/him as a victim of a Eurocentric discursive and cognitive violence. For, in actual fact, Conrad's construction of the African in *Heart of Darkness* is other than the 'Other.' The sense of complementarity which shores up the relationship between the Self and the Other cannot exist in a situation of an absolute negation of that Other. It would be enormously charitable to picture Conrad's African as the true Other of the European, for what does not exist cannot, except by some liberal metaphoric licence, aspire to the alter ego of what does. In Conrad's Africa, the real absent factor is the African.

A practical, incontestible demonstration of this de-humanization and absencing is Conrad's denial to his African that most supremely human of all attributes: language. Africans "howled" and "shrieked" These beings are so rudimentarized by the novelist that their "wild and passionate uproar" never rises to the level of linguistic sublimity. There is sound and noise all right, but no language, no articulatory competence, no discursive command. A pathological silence entraps the 'natives,' as they become, in Toni Morrison's words, "Conrad's unspeaking."[28] Any wonder then that for a definition and articulation of the African's world-view (if she/he is ever credited with any such thing in the novel) we have to rely on the pronouncements of a new Prospero, of another "bud of the nobler race"?

But the real pathology here is Conrad's, a victim of a chronic ethnocentric malaise which springs instant hostility to, and denigration of, what he does not understand. To such afflicted souls, difference (on the other side) is defect, variance is abnormality. Since Conrad never understood, and never considered worth understanding, the linguistic 'peculiarities' of his Africans, whatever language they possessed could not have been anything more than "a violent babble of uncouth sounds." Afterall, his Africans spoke no Polish nor French nor English.

And yet a prevalent, perplexing blindness/silence has fallen on this aspect of Conrad's ethnocentrism in Western criticism. For instance, Brook Thomas makes the very important point that "language is humanity's only access to truth,"[24] but his 'new historicist' project at no time interrogates the denial of that 'access' to Conrad's Africans.

This combination of silence and blindness has characterised Conrad scholarship in the West since the debut of Heart of Darkness. Ross Murfin's case study, despite its post-structuralist aspirations, is no exception. It is noteworthy, for instance, that apart from Brook Thomas who cited Chinua Achebe's thoughtful and seminal essay[25] in his reference, no other contributor to this book showed any awareness of an African response. Even Thomas's magnanimity is limited: although Achebe's essay is listed under "Recent Historical Studies of Conrad"[26], his own new historicist study does not betray even the slightest trace of the content of Achebe's essay. With this process of 'unfair selectivity' and 'preferred visions'[27] late 20th century Western critics have continued Conrad's silencing and negation of Africans. Contemporary Western critics are still co-pilgrims in the steamer up the Congo; for them, the African's humanity still remains a 'thought,' a fragile 'suspicion.'[28]

Either as a result of the politics of their provenance or an inherent crisis in their modes and methods of analysis and application (or both), 'mainstream' Western post-structuralist theories have demonstrated little or no adequacy in the apprehension, analysis, and articulation of African writing and its long and troubled context. This essay is not intended to push an exclusivist, essentialist viewpoint that 'our' literature cannot be apprehended by 'their' theory. But it is the case that the ethnocentric universalism of contemporary theoretical practice; its reification of theory into some oracular Western canonical monologue, its fetishization of text and disregard for the deeper reaches of referentiality, its replacement of theory itself with masochistic theoreticism—all these crises have produced a kind of radical conservatism, an anti-hegemonic hegemony which distance Western theory from the fundamental peculiarities of non-Western peoples.

In many ways, post-structuralist method and tool of analysis lack the depth of perception, cogency of insight, and the clarity of procedure displayed by other theories.[29] Deconstruction, for instance, confuses rather than explains, pontificates instead of interpreting. Its treatment of African literature has demonstrated that 'new' is not necessarily better, and that a project which sounds 'post-colonialist' in intent may turn out to be neo-colonialist, even 're-colonialist' in practice.

The preceding submissions are not another 'anti-theory', anti-rigor campaign, and should not be misconstrued as such. Theories matter. They provide a neat, handy background aid to methodological and analytical procedures. They foster and enhance a reflective globality on issues while sharpening that predictive and speculative capability which facilitates the marriage of imagination and knowledge. So, a critique of one type of theory (in this case post-structuralist variety) should not be mistaken for a negation and rejection of all theories. As post-structuralist theories are beginning to accept, thanks to the New

Historicism, all theories are positional, contingent, connected, even partisan. In their orginary, epistemological, and analytical presumptions, the 'major' literary theories in the world today are exclusivistically Western and oracular. They have yet to demonstrate adequate capability for coping with issues and events in other parts of the world.

TEXT WORSHIP
(Or the deconstructed passport of 'Travelling Theory')

Did you see the text pass this way
In coat and collar and pompous sway
A wizened Canon with the cutest creed
With a temple full of the bravest breed

Did you see the Text on the conference table
Talkative giant of a faddish fable
Pounding the podium, a moustached tyrant
How holy his sin-tax, stupendouly brilliant!

When I woke up this morning the Text was in my room
I aimed at its shadow, it held my broom
It jumped into my wardrobe, turned into a hat
Now I strut the streets with a trendy heart
It opens the door to the fattest jobs
The prettiest journals up for grabs
Arrange your jargon on a glittering rack
Your feet are firm on the tenure track

Post-day post-night
Post-history post-reason
Post-humanist post-human
Show me the post of your post-coloniality

Aporia comporia catachresis
Totalizing razmatizzing
Meto nym nym logocentri tri tri
Show me the structure of your post-structurality

Oh for a gram of Grammatogy!
A sample sperm of Disseminations
The Discourse tree with fruits of Discord

And the New His-story-cism, New Her-story-cism

The madder the smatter, the harder the better
Make it new, make it arcane
The clumsier the code the sweeter the pain
It's the brave new era of the gaudy patter

Signs are here, the Word is dead:
The funeral of meaning a tropical debt
Paid in the surface of an idle game
In the dim-lit abyss of pedantic fame

Wars may rage, Hunger may spread
The river may die in its lowly bed
Chains may descend from every sky
The price of Freedom raised so high

Count your tropes, praise the Text
The meaningless meaning is a grand pretext
'Oppression' is merely undecidable reference
'Poverty' is slave to metaphysics of presence

The Author is dead, in unmarked grave dumped
The Reader to power with crown has rumped
The Text writes itself with a magic hand
In the curious way its priests can stand

It shouts in French, in English it whispers
It murmurs in German in gasps and whimpers
A Kingly silence in other tongues
The youngest heir to older wrongs

I bend my knee, oh mighty Text
Spare my days of your nightly test
Assure my path to your Temple of Awe
Let me rant while my listeners snore

Notes

1. See Biodun Jeyifo, "Decolonizing Theory: Reconceptualizating the New English Literatures". Paper presented at the 1990 M.L.A. annual conference, Chicago, U.S.A., p.2

2. Cited in Firinne Chreachain, "'Post-Colonialism' or Second Independence?", African Literature Association Bulletin, Vol. 17, No. 3, 1991 pp. 5-6.

3. Ibid., p. 5.

4. Biodun Jeyifo, op. cit., p. 2.

5. Rashimi Bhatnager, Lola Chatterjee and Rajeshwari Sunder Rajan, "The Post-Colonial Critic" (Interview with Gayatri Spivak) in Sarah Harasym (ed.), *The Post-colonial Critic: Interviews, Strategies, Dialogues.* New York and London: Routledge, p. 69.

6. Bill Ashcroft, Gareth Griffiths, and Helen Tiffin, *The Empire Writes Back: Theory and Practice in Post-Colonial Literatures.* London and New York: Routledge, 1989, p. 2.

7. Bill Ashcroft et al., Ibid.

8. Biodun Jeyifo, op. cit., p. 2.

9. Ross Murfin (ed.), Joseph Conrad, *Heart of Darkness: A Case Study in Contemporary Criticism.* New York: St. Martin's Press, 1989.

10. All page references to the Ross Murfin edition of *Heart of Darkness* abbreviated here as H.O.D.

11. Adena Rosmarin, "Darkening the Reader: Reader-Response Criticism and Heart of Darkness" in Murfin (ed.), *Joseph Conrad, Heart of Darkness: A Case Study in Contemporary Criticism*, p. 155.

12. Adena Rosemarin, Ibid., p. 15.

13. Adena Rosemarin, Ibid.

14. *Heart of Darkness* (Ross Murfin Edition), p. 60.

15. Ross Murfin, in Ross Murfin (ed.), *Joseph Conrad, Heart of Darkness: A Case Study in Contemporary Criticism*, p. 226.

16. Ross Murfin, Ibid.

17. Brook Thomas, "Preserving and Keeping Order by Killing Time in Heart of Darkness", in Ross Murfin (ed.), Ibid., pp. 237-258.

18. Brook Thomas, Ibid., p. 337.

19. Brook Thomas, Ibid., p. 248.

20. Brook Thomas, Ibid., p. 251.

21. Quoted by Brook Thomas, Ibid., p. 242.

22. Brook Thomas, Ibid., p. 245.

23. Toni Morrison, "Unspeakable Things Unspoken: The Afro-American Presence in American Literature," Michigan Quarterly Review, Vol. XXVIII, No. 1, 1989, p. 9.

24. Brook Thomas, op. cit., p. 250.

25. Chinua Achebe, "An Image of Africa: Racism in Conrad's Heart of Darkness, in *Hopes and Impediments: Selected Essays.* New York: Doubleday 1989, pp. 1-20.

26. Brook Thomas, op. cit., p. 257.
27. Biodun Jeyifo, "For Chinua Achebe: The Resilience and Predicament of Obierika," manuscript, 1990, p. 10.
28. For further demonstration of this attitude, see readers' responses to Gerald Graff's very significant article, "What Has Literary Theory Wrought?", *The Chronicle of Higher Education*, February 12, 1992, P.A. 48, in the March 11, 1992 issue of the same periodical, p. 84.
29. Niyi Osundare, "An Empty Technology of the Text?: Deconstruction and African Literature", Unpublished manuscript.

*SINGERS OF A NEW DAWN: NIGERIAN LITERATURE FROM THE SECOND GENERATION ON

I

Let me begin by congratulating the organisers of this conference on devoting a respectable portion of their deliberations to Nigerian literature. And I would like to assure you that there is nothing patronising or gratuitous about my sentiment. On the contrary, it is a feeling borne of delight and surprise. For, before my invitation to this conference arrived a few months ago, I was beginning to nurse a secret fear that the West, especially Europe, was losing interest in African literature and its embattled creators. Could this be due to the termination of the Cold War (and the beginning of the "End of History," as some hasty historiographers would like to call it); is it traceable to the end of apartheid and the several anti-apartheid conferences which afforded some people in the West the opportunity of demonstrating their solidarity with the victims of that monster;

or is it due to the general "Africa fatigue" which the West is suspected to be suffering as a result of the continent's "basket case" and its unending catalogue of woes? In other words, has the West now got so terribly bogged down by the pogroms in Rwanda, anarchy in Liberia and Somalia, the murderous dictatorships which hold down several African countries in cruel thraldom, that it has very little time and space left for African literature, for African culture? Or is that literature thought to have perished in the maelstrom of Africa's perennial catastrophes? What has become of the enthusiasm, insight, and energy with which Europe embraced African literature in the sixties and seventies?

So many questions. So much anxiety. How else can the Empire write back if not through a scroll of queries and riddles? Othered into marginality, Africa remains the perpetual periphery, a zone of turbuent silence and abysmal distance. But in that zone is the vortex of angst and argument, deep-seated whimpers and muffled articulations. To speak and not be heard, or rather, to speak and be denied audience is a kind of silenc(e)ing that may sometimes be damning and downright censorious in its impact. There is always something unwholesome about neglect, whether benign or malignant.

The point I am trying to make is that the theory (and practice) of unequal exchange which has always characterised relations between Africa and the West, and which has hitherto been seen largely in economic terms, is even more pernicious at the cultural-literary level. The general feeling among writers and scholars on the other side of the Mediterranean where I come from is that Africa knows so much about the literature of the West, while the West knows so little about the literature of Africa. And the absence of reciprocity is the bane of any relationship; it hurts both parties by negating the possibility of wholesome exchange.

Take a comparative look at the literature curricula on both sides and a disturbing one-sidedness leaps to the fore. For instance, no student can obtain a degree in literature (even in English) in a Nigerian university without studying Shakespeare, Chaucer, Hardy, Elliot, Faulkner, Melville; without some knowledge of Racine, Moliere, Tolstoy, Chekov; without more than a passing acquaintance with Brecht, Heidegger, Goethe, Nietzsche, Mann; without due genuflection at the altar of Foucault, Lyotard, Derrida and other high priests of the "post-" theology.

Consider the situation on the other side of the Mediterranean where African literature is still some unknown beast in many universities and colleges, and you get the picture of a story standing precariously on one leg. Put yourself in the position of your African counterpart, and you feel the weight of a career devoted to studying the literature (and culture) of others who care very little about your own. Beyond the strict confines of literature, the music of Bach, Beethoven, Wagner, etc. wax triumphantly in concert halls, churches, schools, and private homes, relished for their indisputable virtuosity and charm. But then you ask: is African music received and appreciated with anything near equal enthusiasm and interest in Europe and America?

I am of the considered opinion that for a genuine literary (qua cultural) exchange to take place, the West will have to expand its reading list to accommodate works from Africa and other parts of the globe handily but disturbingly referred to as the "Third World." Now, I am not unaware of the on-going "canon war" which is in many ways a literary, intellectual front in the battle against multiculturalism. To many pundits of the ivory tower and the political podium the opening up of Western culture for much-needed ventillation and enrichment by other cultures is regarded as treacherous invasion, a prelude to the dilution of an autolectic High Culture and its Classical patrimony. Hence liberal literature teachers and curriculum developers have to spend endless time justifying the inclusion of Wole Soyinka and Chinua Achebe in a reading list which regards Thomas Mann and Thomas Hardy as natural, legitimate "canons." The last pair is not only "canonical"; it is also "universal," authors of "travelling" texts and facilitators of the "travelling" theories generated around them. It is, of course, to be assumed that these texts carry Western passports fortified by Western visas which guarantee free, privileged passage across the globe. The question still begging for an answer is why texts bearing the passport of other parts of the world find it so difficult to "travel" through the delicate terrain of Europe and America.

Almost invariably, our attitude to literature and its canons is a reflection of the prevailing political situation and its myriad anxieties. Isn't there a link between the present canon worship and the embattlement of multiculturalism in academe, and the socio-political closure which manifests itself in increasing racism and more severe immigration laws? A new exclusivist ethos pervades the streets, with busy allies in absolutism and zenophobia, erecting new walls, hardening the discursive highway into a supra-monologic cul de sac. And hereby comes the relevance of literature, its plural possibilities and healing power. For literature matters, it matters crucially. This is an old point worth belaboring in a "post-this," "post-that" age when the word has been deconstructed into indeterminate meaninglessness, and literature gasps in the hothouse of cavalier signs and vacuous significations. As I said before another audience in Japan last year,

> ...true literature is...transgressive of negative limits: it subverts artificial borders, scales iron fences, breaks down walls. It interrogates oppressive customs, strives for the uplift of the human spirit, seeks authentic cultivation. It goes beyond a mere renovation of the human spirit; it insists on wholesome renewal.[1]

II

In stressing so passionately the moral and communal imperatives of literature, am I not sounding like a warrior from a forgotten age? In thus evoking the literary enterprise as a shared, answerable phenomenon, where do I really belong in an era of solipsistic theorizing and indeterminate textualities? Well, like the masquerade which surfaces in the street of another village, my costume tells my distant origins, my song the wisdom issuing out of a particular soil. What I have said so far provides a hint for the preoccupations of Nigerian literature, its bold, responsive tenor, its sense of place, its constant search for that meeting point between the beautiful and the useful.

Nigeria is a place where literature still matters, where people still ask at the end of the story: 'alright, what does this tale teach us?' It is a place where authorship carries a grave, sometimes tragic, responsibility; a place where a story, a poem, an essay, even an innocent metaphor may provoke the dictator's wrath and lead straight on to a spell in a dreary dungeon. Those who doubt this fact should remember the recent hanging of Ken Saro Wiwa, the poet, novelist, dramatist, essayist, polemicist, and publisher who committed his vast literary talents to the pursuit of social justice. A sense of the writer's responsibility and the social and cultural answerability of his/her art have been kept in the forefront since the beginning of modern written Nigerian literature. In a now famous essay written over three decades ago, Chinua Achebe described the novelist as teacher and went on to justify the social responsibilities of art.[2] About two years later, Wole Soyinka typified the writer as "the voice of vision in his own time."[3] The views of these pioneers have turned out to be enduring: the older the country has grown, the more intimidating have been its problems, the more inevitable has been the writer's mission as prophet, gadfly, critic—and martyr.

Nigerian literature has a common grounding, a certain organizing principle, a universe of common fears and shared aspirations. But like the country whose voice it is striving to be, that literature is also polyphonic, heterogeneous, vigorous and turbulent. Like the country, it is sweet and sour, energized by a baffling complexity, paradox and irony. But unlike the country Nigeria, Nigerian literature possesses–has developed–a binding, overwhelming sense of mission and a humanist vision tragically absent in the country's political domain. Thus while we can reasonably talk about the nationhood of our letters, the praxis of nationhood or nation-ness at the political level remains a moot point.

In other words, the visionary thrust of Nigerian literature is way ahead of the country's social and political reality. Any wonder, then, that the writers are so impatient with their country's millennial crawl; any wonder that they are frequently at loggerheads with functionaries–whether military or civilian–at the helm of political affairs?

Denizens of dawn, singers of a new day–these are what Nigerian writers have always strived to be. From the first generation of Ekwensi, Achebe, Soyinka, Okigbo, Clarke-Bekederemo, Segun, Aluko, Okara, Nwapa, Munonye, Ike, Amadi, Sofola, Rotimi (forgive me: name-dropping is inevitable in an address of this type!), Nigerian writers have never shied away from a vociferous engagement with the country's destiny. Styles and perspectives, levels of engagement differ, of course, as do temperaments and personal loyalties. But these writers come under a broad ideological umbrella; they are members of a comity of common interests.

The above category of writers is not the focus of this address, for the simple (even if inadequate) reason that they have been around for so long, and I assume that I can credit this audience with a reasonable familiarity with their works. But in this case, omission is by no means the same thing as absence: we shall see below how the influences and echoes of these pioneers resonate in the works of their successors from the second generation on.

The generation after that of Achebe and Soyinka can justifiably be called the angry generation. Born immediately after the Second World War, they lived their early years through colonialism and the struggle for independence. They watched the euphoria of that achievement dip into the massive disillusionment of the post-independence period during which Nigerian's fledgling democracy tottered into a military dictatorship, then a series of coups and counter-coups, bloody ethnic hostilities, and a wasteful civil war. They watched the sun of independence disappear behind the clouds, even as long-cherished values collapsed and the country staggered into a "season of anomy." This generation absorbed these turmoils in their impressionable years; many of them suffered or even perished in the civil war and the various crises which served as its prelude. They thus grew up an angry generation: a righteous rage seethed through their lines.

But it was a literate, regenerative kind of anger. Unlike, or much more than, their predecessors, this generation took advantage of revolutionary Marxism whose radical theory and praxis were considered suitable for their analyses and apprehension of the African situation.[4] They dreamed new dreams, and were quick to point out alternative visions of a truly just and egalitarian society. For the first time, names such as Sartre, Benjamin, Lukacs, Althusser, Fanon, de Beauvoir, Cabral, etc. featured frequently in university lectures and conference circuits. Bertolt Brecht leapt to the Nigerian stage, and dramatists like Osofisan, Osanyin, and Obafemi endowed him with an indigenous mask and meaning.

A new aesthetic accompanied these developments. A new sense of cultural authenticity emerged, people-oriented, firmly rooted, but without the soporific nostalgia of Senghorian Negritudism. There was an active, unpatronising re-evaluation of folklore and the oral tradition, and an appropriation of its salient stylistic strategies. This was not only an angry generation; it was also a generation in a hurry to touch the people, to *affect* their lives. They are a generation with a live coal in their palm: they have no time for *iregbe* (dilly dally, idleness).

Perhaps no other literary genre expresses the above characteristics more palpably, more consistently than poetry (which also produces by far the largest number of practitioners of all the genres). A confident sense of purpose, an unmistakable degree of audience-consciousness inform the practice of the poets of this generation. In a much-cited "Prologue..." to *The Poet Lied*, Odia Ofeimun asserts:

> I have come down
> to tell my story
> by the same fireside
> around which
> my people are gathered
>
> I have come home
> to feel for ears and hearts and hands
> to rise with me
> when I say the words
> of my mouth

> And I must tell my story
> to nudge and awaken them
> that sleep
> among my people[5]

Evident here is an attempt to build a bridge between "I" and "my people", between "my mouth" and their "ears", thus creating a strong communal bond. The "fireside" becomes a metaphoric *locus dramatis* whose earthy impact is underscored by the word "home" in the second stanza. The last stanza leaves us in no doubt as to the poet's belief in the revolutionary power of poetry. A similar sense of the functional artistic self pervades the arena when, in *What the Madman Said*, Obiora Udechukwu's persona declares:

> I am the one speaking!
> If I do not wake the cock,
> The cock will not wake the sun[6]

Note, again, the assertive first person pronoun, the transformation from sleep into awakening, lethargy into action. In the songs of Tanure Ojaide, these resolves take on a lyrical ring:

> I sing with a full throat of my mother, my land.
> I sing of the hidden spirit of our midst,
> I sing of the redeemer in the womb of time,
> I sing of the revolution incubating in the heart,
> I sing of the pain before delivery[7]

Hand in hand with this urgency of purpose is a deliberate stylistic accessibility. Hardly would you find instances of Soyinka's profusely elliptical syntax in the poetry of this generation; hardly Okigbo's hauntingly lyrical but punishing hermetic flamboyance. As a matter of fact, it was a reaction to the exclusivist obscurity of the Okigbo generation that inspired the opening poem in my first collection:

Poetry is
not the esoteric whisper
of an excluding tongue
not a claptrap
for a wondering audience
not a learned quiz
entombed in Grecoroman lore[8]

The eighties witnessed a robust flowering of Nigerian poetry in English. Creative writing courses sprang up in many Nigerian universities; so did poetry clubs which organized literary competitions and frequent readings. There was a successful attempt to take poetry from the closet to the marketplace, from the classroom to the public forum. "Poet's Corners" surfaced in many newspapers and magazines.[9] This period witnessed the publication of Molara Ogundipe-Leslie's *Sew the Old Days*, Femi Fatoba's *Petals of Thought*, Funso Aiyejina's *Letter to Lynda*, Ada Ugah's *Songs of the Talakawa*, Harry Garuba's *Shadow and Dream*, Ossie Enekwe's *Broken Pot*, Ezenwa Ohaeto's *Songs of a Traveller*, Livinus Odozor's *Songs of the Bayonet Man*. It was also this decade that the "Update Poets"[10] made their remarkable debut.

A robustness of spirit, a variety of masks, a sensitive, controversial topicality,—these have remained the hallmark of modern Nigerian theatre since Soyinka's pioneering efforts in the sixties. But unlike Okigbo and J. P. Clarke-Bekederemo in poetry, Soyinka has not produced a multitude of successors in drama. Femi Osofisan, Bode Sowande, Tess Onwueme, Sam Ukala, Bode Osanyin, Olu Obafemi, Stella Oyedepo, Akanji Nasiru[11] have been active on the Nigerian stage, though it must be admitted that modern Nigerian theatre still remains a university-based phenomenon. However, location has not been allowed to constitute a barrier to visionary outreach. Like the poets discussed earlier on, these dramatists confront the social ills of contemporary Nigeria—socio-economic and political oppression, corruption, tribalism, gender inequality, etc.—in an idiom that is simple and deliberately direct. Notable in these regards are Sowande's *Farewell to Babylon* and *Tornadoes Full of Dreams*, Okala's *The Slave Wife* and *The Log in Your Eye*,

Obafemi's *Suicide Syndrome* and *Naira Has No Gender*, Nasiru's *Our Survival*.

In many ways, the works of Femi Osofisan and Tess Onwueme typify two significant tendencies in the drama of the generation under review. In sheer versatility, prolificity, and knack for frequent experimentation, Osofisan's output can be seen as both model and representative of this generation. His is the theater of parables, of controversy and polemic, of deeply probed problems and problematic solutions.

Rooted and frequently profound, Osofisan arrives with the best in the marriage between traditional African theatrical modes and Western dramaturgic strategies. His early works were more obviously influenced by Bertolt Brecht, but as I said earlier on, he endowed that European genius with an African mask and a native idiom. Constant in Osofisan's project is the vision of a new society, a clear alternative to our present nightmare. But in the pursuit of that ideal, skepticism sometimes hardens into anxiety, animating that grey zone between optimism and despair. This is the problem with plays like *Aringindin* and *Oriki of a Grasshopper* in which helplessness tends to take the place of confident affirmation—a far cry from the positive ebullience of *The Chattering of the Song* or the revolutionary fervour of *Morountodun*.

A deep humanist ethos runs through Osofisan's drama, sensitive and urgently engaging. Compassion, an increasingly rare virtue in this "post-modernist" world, comes centre stage in *Eshu and the Vagabond Minstrels*, while the question of power, its use and abuse, assumes central focus in *Yungbayungba*. In *Nkrumah Ni*, about his most ambitious play to date, Osofisan reenacts a significant segment of the life (and times) of one of Africa's most momentous personalities of the 20th century. A bold, painstaking effort which has benefitted greatly from the introduction of chorus-jesters and that ingeniously symbolic lawn tennis court exchange, *Nkrumah Ni* takes us through a complex web of memory and ideas, power and passion. But overall, while the stage Cabral comes quite close to the compassionate original, Nkrumah is somewhat flat, Sekou Toure frenetic almost to the point of dementia.

Ready-made characters come with ready-made problems. In the case of *Nkrumah Ni*, the characters are so monumental that the stage trembles under their feet. How does one place a mask on a face already so starkly famous? How does one create fiction out of long-established facts without doing violence to the tenets of credibility? Osofisan has grappled with these problems and more, but the result could have been more satisfying, more convincing. Needed here is that magic which transformed Moremi from a mytho-historical figure into a compelling stage presence. Osofisan's oeuvre is rich and impressive, his thematic preoccupations wide and rather complex. Like most sensitive artists in a demonically oppressive country like Nigeria, his sensibility has its peaks and lows. But noteworthy in his works is the theme of the usefulness of anger and the inevitability of change. Let Leje complete the story:

> but seasons change, oppression
> and injustice resurface in new forms,
> and new weapons have to be
> devised to eliminate them[12]

Like Osofisan's , Tess Onwueme's theater is a marketplace of ideas and ideals. Issues of social inequality, political oppression, racism, ageism dominate her drama from the apprentice pieces such as *A Hen Too Soon, Ban Empty Barn,* to the fairly executed ones like *The Desert Encroaches* and *Legacies.* There is a relentless search for roots and origins, a passionate crusade against those who "Anglicize our language" and "Black-out the black past" (1989:48). In *Legacies* Onwueme warns against the danger of Westernization without modernization, the death of the self which accompanies the Black person's loss of identity. There is a crucial diasporic thrust in this play: every Black separated from Africa by slavery carries a half *ikenga* crying to be re-united with the other half in a final rite of retrieval and arrival.

In many ways *Legacies* serves as a kind of fore-runner to *Tell it to Women,* by far the most accomplished of Onwueme's plays so far. The author has christened this play as "an Epic Drama for Women." And justifiably so. This is a play in which women occupy center stage and men have to peep from the wings. The well-primed satirical barbs descend on three major but related targets: feminism, First Ladyism, and urban-rural disparities. Onwueme's strong dislike for Western-type feminism is symbolized "Dr. Ruth" (p. 103), a bookish, soulless, deracinated feminist terrorist who "dish(es) out dogmas in such large doses" (p. 107). Onwueme does not see the way to women's liberation in Ruth's kind of man-hating, family-wrecking ideology; for motherhood, which this ideology sees as a yoke, is for woman a source of supreme power.[13] The womanist perspective espoused by this play is the type which embraces rootedness and societal harmony, and the "cooperative ideal."[14]

Onwueme is candid enough to admit that some of the greatest enemies of the woman's cause are women themselves. Consider the arrogant, squandermaniac First Lady, her Better Life for Rural Women Programme, and her cruel exploitation of poor rural folks whom she knows so little about. Consider the overbearing mother-in-law who keeps insisting that her son's wife must produce male children. On the other side is Yemoja, the solid bond between opposing parties, Adaku the ideational and rhetorical pillar of the play, and Bose who dances into a future more authentic than the past in which she was born.

Tell It To Women is a telling account, a speech arena and theater of discursive engagement. This play is neater and better expressed than any other by Tess Onwueme. The wisdom and eloquence of Adaku are truly remarkable, bringing lurid echoes of the Old Man from Abafon in Achebe's *Anthills of the Savannah*. But there are significant problems. Some of the movements are too wordy, some stage directions read like long passages from a novel, while the play as a whole could do without a third of its present size. Generally Onwueme's defence of traditional African values is sound and re-assuring, but her plays are marked by avoidable anthropologism.

The same audience-consciousness, the same communicative impulse, the same passionate engagement with social issues, which we have witnessed in the first two genres also feature prominently in prose fiction. Next to poetry, the story-tellers' club boasts the largest membership in Nigeria. And it is also a genre espousing a variety of ideological-stylistic tendencies:

socialist-realist (Omotoso, Iyayi, Okoye); critical-realist (Saro-Wiwa, Okpewho, Okri, Iroh, Emecheta, Omowunmi Segun, Eno Obong, Okediran, Mowah, Oyegoke, Areo, Omobowale, Otiono; magical-realist the latter Ben Okri, Biyi Bandele-Thomas); womanist/feminist (Alkali, Emecheta, Okoye, Omowunmi Segun, Eno Obong); factive, that is, fact + fiction (Omotoso, Adenubi).

This is a rich, thronged club, but for the sake of brevity I can only consider a few names. Festus Iyayi stands out in this group both in terms of the quantity of his output and the sheer relevance of his vision. A simple, almost elemental story-teller not known for the piquant wit and earthy satire of Ken Saro Wiwa, nor the elaborate plot structure of Okpewho, Iyayi is unsparing in his excoriation of evil and vindication of goodness. Just like Osofisan and Omotoso, this novelist forces us into a re-appraisal of heroship and our traditional conception of it. This is one of Iyayi's missions in the aptly titled *Heroes,* a novel which presents the "little man" as the real hero of the Nigerian civil war, contrary to the purple chronicles and boastful claims of generals and overbearing functionaries. In his first and, to my mind, most engaging novel *Violence*, Iyayi presents a touching but unsentimental picture of Idemudia and others like him who are forced to sell their very blood in order to stay alive. But always, in Iyayi hope survives; justice cuts a path to the future.

With Ifeoma Okoye, Zaynab Alkali, and Eno Obong, we arrive at the gendered juncture. Reacting against a largely patriarchal society which has marginalized woman for so long, they have created works of fiction in which woman is both center and subject of the discursive universe. Woman is now teller of her own tale, no longer the conspicuous absence in *Things Fall Apart,* the prostitute in *Jagua Nana*, nor the airy, mystical presence in *Season of Anomy*. Pressing issues burn through the pages: the problems of childlessness, polygamy, marital infidelity, male impotence, male child syndrome, mother-in-lawism, religious restriction. And, of course, in the background always is Nigeria's blighted socio-political system which has turned the majority of the citizens into slaves, and women into more pathetic slaves.

The issue of childlessness, for instance, is not new in Nigerian literature. It is a recurrent trope in folktales, and a prominent theme in Flora Nwapa, the first Nigerian female novelist. Always it is the woman who gets the blame in a childless marriage. She is so easily, so comfortably presumed to be the empty vessel, the one that cannot perform. But Okoye in *Behind the Clouds* and Alkali in *The Stillborn* locate the source of this problem in men. In the former novel, the sterile Dozie "cocky in his ignorance"[15] learns to his utter dismay that he is, indeed, the problem. Fortunately modern medicine comes in as *deus-ex-machina*: Dozie gets a cure, and together he and his wife begin the process of building and rehabilitation. The idea of couples building together receives focal attention in Eno Obong's *Garden House*, by far one of the most accomplished but one of the least discussed novels to have come out Nigeria in the last decade.

Mayen, the rapturously beautiful Mammywata figure, dominates the story. Her first marriage to Kabiri, the bigoted wheeler-dealer collapses, as does his glass-and-stone house whose whole essence is vulgar and foreign. But her union with Wande Adebo, architect and geologist, marks the beginning of restoration and renewal. Together they think, and dream, and talk and plan their new garden house, an architectural beauty in the center of the country, full of love, alive with bliss.

Nigerian prose fiction has explored the country's turbulent terrain over the years. But I cannot conclude this section of my survey without a brief mention of prose *faction*, a new sub-genre which permits a liberal cohabitation of fact and fiction under the same narrative roof. The first major instance of this was Soyinka's *Ake;* later on came *Isara* and *Ibadan*. But if Soyinka's faction has a strong autobiographical base, Kole Omotoso's *Just Before Dawn* is the history—no, narrative of Nigeria's story—with tremendous artistic liberty and visionary reconstruction, while Mobolaji Adenubi's *Splendid* reads like a thrilling mix of biography and history with a delicate touch of the novelistic style. In a new, exciting way, Omotoso went back to Nigeria's past to find a way to the country's future.

III

"I am a child of the war", declares Olu Oguibe, "I have bitterness in my blood".[16] No epigram can be more fitting for the young generation of Nigerian writers among whom Oguibe, a sensitive, committed, and versatile artist, forms a significant part. This is a generation born around Nigeria's independence (1960), Nigeria's midnight children, as it were, who have spent the first three decades of their lives confronting the nightmare that the country has become. If the second generation we have just discussed can be described as angry, the temperament of the new generation ranges from angry through desperate to despondent. This is a generation which attained adolescence in the oil boom years, dipping into poverty and unemployment a few years later as the country went from boom to bust. A generation whose dreams collapsed so rapidly that many of them are wont to lament with Oguibe: "I have aged in my youth."[17]

It is also a generation of deep-seated anxieties. Permit me to quote from a personal letter which accompanied "A Grave November," a series of poems recently sent to me by Ademola Babajide, one of the most lyrical poets of the new generation. The immediate inspiration for the poems was the hanging of Ken Saro Wiwa last November:

> I was nothing short of anarchy in ferment then. I mean how does one react to a gang of bandits desecrating the very earth in which one is rooted, and by so doing defiling the very meaning of one's existence?... If I am still alive by then (another decade) I will be 45—the ploughing days all gone. So what fruits, what harvest should one expect from such a season?

There are other sources of anxiety. The writing career of this generation coincided with the virtual collapse of the publishing industry in Nigeria as a result of a serious economic recession, itself the repercussion of a grossly mismanaged economy. Many good manuscripts are therefore ageing and gathering dust in their writers' drawers. All this notwithstanding, a fair number of titles has managed to hit the shelves, thanks to the emergence of small-scale indigenous publishing outfits which have remained active on the literary scene in the past decade or so. The quality of production as well as that of the text has been anything but even, but we have been saved the horror of an absolute silence in the literary arena.

The generation under review can aptly be described as the poets' generation. Close to three quarters of its publications belong to the poetic genre, and names such as the following are beginning to establish themselves on the Nigerian literary scene: Femi Oyebode, Olu Oguibe, Afam Akeh, Ogaga Ifowodo, Esiaba Irobi, Onookome Okome, Uche Nduka, Chiedu Ezeanah, Usman Shehu, Kemi Atanda-Ilori, Izzia Ahmad, Sesan Ajayi, Remi Raji, Sola Osofisan, Nnimmo Bassey, Toyin Adewale-Nduka, Obu Udeozo, Eddie Aderinokun, Kayode Aderinokun, Joe Ushie, Maik Nwosu, Epaphras Osondu, Obi Nwakanma, Asodionye Ejiofor, Tunde Olusunle, Wunmi Raji, Isidore Diala, Ogechi Iromantu. A large, many-tenored clan, but individual voices are becoming discernible: the learned, allusive style of Oyebode and Irobi; the bardic, orature-powered flamboyance of Oguibe, Nwosu, Babajide; the wry epigrammatism of Akeh; the clamorous satiricality of Bassey, Ushie, Olusunle; the soft, feminine affirmativeness of Adewale-Nduka. A pageant of voices less ideologically conscious than the second generation, but busy devising their own means of confronting the Nigerian monster.

A generation heavy on poetry, lean on prose, but the achievements of Omowunmi Segun, Karen King-Aribisala, Nduka Otiono, Nwachukwu-Agbada; the promise of Sanya Osha, Akin Adesokan, and several others whose manuscripts have yet to transform into books, have created an inescapable debate on the Nigerian literary scene. In a quietly satirical vein, Segun locks us in combat once again with high-level corruption in Nigeria, while a significant strand in her tale brings us face to face with some of the lingering repercussions of the civil war. King-Aribisala is the keen-eyed, unsparing satirist, while Otiono's best stories take us forcibly back to "what happens to narrative as it travels from the oral to the written form" (Foreword). In a generation, some of whose members evince a certain strain of alienation, Otiono's confidence in his oral roots is quite re-assuring. There is certainly more to be said about this unfolding generation. In the meantime let Ezenwa Ohaeto who tells "the story of tomorrow's dawn"[18] now have the last say:

> Is God now tired of this land?
> I must go to see God
> before God goes to bed.[19]

The Night Masquerade knows that for the real "cleansing" to take place, his has to be "a generation of sacrifice."[20]

IV

From my observations above we can see that Nigerian literature is diverse, complex and highly responsive. It is a literature which takes the bull by the horns, one which is never afraid of telling the emperor that indeed, he is naked. Nigeria is a sorely abused country, constantly trampled and wasted by insensitive rulers. But always the writer proffers the healing hand, points out alternative visions. My emphasis has been on the "angry" second generation and the "anxious" generation after them. These are generations stung into creativity by Nigeria's nightmare, but which have refused to give up on the country. Generations whose tornadoes are full of dreams.[21] Permit me to end this address, therefore, with a "dream" from *Midlife*, a volume composed around my fortieth birthday:

> I behold
>
> Stubborn roots in league
> against the sickle's insistence
>
> The fireflames of mountains
> which burn with volcanic splendour
>
> I behold

The unwinding loincloths of men who play god
in temples of wooden angels

The deciduous laughter
of eating chiefs

I behold

The heaviness of the needle,
the weightless truth of fractured visions

The ringing alpha of concluded minds,
the sprouting song of buried virtues

I behold

The plough's glare in the mirror
of the preening soil

seasons stark drunk
on the talent of the grape

I behold

Stars marching back to claim
the patrimony of the night

The revelry of the new moon,
thunder's laughter in the comedy of the sky

I behold

Touching boulders,
The sympathy of stone.

Clouds which full-fill
the promise of rain.[22]

* Keynote address, Anglestentag: Conference of German Professors of English, Dresden, Germany, October 1, 1996.

Notes

1. Niyi Osundare, "Literature as a Medium of Cultural Exchange: The African Example". Address at the Japan-Africa Forum, Nagoya, Japan, 1995, p. 11.
2. Chinua Achebe, "The Novelist as Teacher", *Morning Yet on Creation Day*. London: Heinemann, 1975, pp. 42-45.
3. Wole Soyinka, "The Writer in a Modern African State", *The Writer in Modern Africa*, ed. Per Wastberg. Uppsala: Scandinavian Institute of African Studies, 1968.
4. Femi Osfisan, "Warriors of a Failed Utopia? West African Writers Since the 70's". 2nd Annual African Studies Lecture, Institute of African Studies, University of Leeds, U.K., 1996.
5. Odia Ofeimun, *The Poet Lied*. Lagos: Update Communications, 1989, p. 1.
6. Obiora Udechukwu, *What the Madman Said*. Bayreuth: Boomerang Press, 1990, p. 49.
7. Tanure Ojaide, *Labyrinths of the Delta*. New York: The Greenfield Review Press, 1986, p. 79.
8. Niyi Osundare, *Songs of the Marketplace*. Ibadan: New Horn Press, 1983, p. 3.
9. I was part of this poetic outreach, having run a regular poetry column in the *Sunday Tribune* (Nigeria) from 1985-1990. For a brief account of my experience on that experiment, see S. Arnold and A. Nitecki, eds., *Culture and Development in Africa*. Trenton, New Jersey: Africa World Press, 1990, pp. 1-47.

10. Afam Akeh, Izzia Ahmad, Kemi Atanda-Ilori, Esiaba Irobi, and Uche Nduka.
11. Zulu Sofola and Ola Rotimi do not fall within this category though they have strong stylistic affinities with its members: for instance, Rotimi and Osofisan; Sofola and Onwueme.
12. Femi Osofisan, *The Chattering and the Song*. Ibadan: Ibadan University Press, 1976, p. 54.
13. See Catherine Acholonu, *Motherism, the Afrocentric Alternative to Feminism*. Owerri: Afa Publications, 1995.
14. Chikwenye Ogunyemi, *Africa Wo/Man Palava: The Nigerian Novel by Women*. Chicago & London: The University of Chicago Press, 1996, p. 306.
15. Ogunyemi, p. 303.
16. Olu Oguibe, *A Gathering Fear*. Ibadan: Kraft Books, 1992, p. 91.
17. Oguibe, p. 17.
18. Ezenwa Ohaeto, *The Voice of the Night Masquerade*. Ibadan: Kraft Books, 1996, p. 82.
19. Ohaeto, p. 24.
20. Ohaeto, p. 20.
21. Bode Sowande, *Tornadoes Full of Dreams*. Lagos: Malthouse Press, 1990.
22. Niyi Osundare, *Midlife*. Ibadan: Heinemann Educational Books, 1993, pp. 106-107.

Literary works mentioned in the text

Acholonu, C. *The Spring's Last Drop*. Owerri: Totan Publishers, 1985.
Adenubi, M. *Splendid*. Ibadan: Spectrum Books, 1995.
Aderinokun, E. *Indigo Tears*. Lagos: Service & Service Publishers, 1992.

Aderinokun, E. *Milestones.* Lagos: Service & Service Publishers, 1995

Aderinokun, K. (1995). *Inferno in the Rain.* Lagos & Ibadan: S & S Publication, 1995.

Adewale-Nduka, T. *Naked Testimonies.* Lagos: Mace Associates Ltd.,1995.

Aiyejina, F. *A Letter to Lynda.* Port Harcourt: Saros International Publishers, 1988.

Ajayi, S. *A Burst of Fireflies.* Ibadan: Kraft Books Ltd., 1992.

Akeh, A. *Stolen Moments.* Lagos: Update Communications Ltd., 1988.

Alkali, S. *The Stillborn.* Lagos: Longman, 1984.

Areo, A. *Paradise for the Masses.* Lagos: Paperback Publishers, 1985

Atanda-Ilori, K. *Amnesty.* Lagos, Update Communications Ltd., 1988.

Babajide, A. *A Grave November.* Manuscript., 1996

Bassey, N. *Patriots and Cockroaches.* Ibadan: Kraft Books Ltd., 1992.

Bassey, N. *Poems on the Run.* Ibadan: Kraft Books Ltd., 1995.

Enekwe, O. O. *Broken Pots.* Nsukka: Afa Press, 1986.

Fatoba, F. *Petals of Thought.* London: New Beacon Press, 1984.

Garuba, H. *Shadow and Dream.* Ibadan: New Horn Press, 1982.

Ifowodo, O. *Homeland and Other Poems.* Ibadan: Kraft Books Ltd., 1998.

Iyayi, F. *Violence.* Longman, 1979.

Iyayi, F.. *Heroes.* Longman, 1987.

Irobi, E. *Cotyledons.* Lagos: Update Communication Ltd., 1988.

Iromantu, O. *Outpouring of Innocence.* Lagos: Pulse Communications, 1995.

King-Aribisala, K. *Our Wife*. Lagos: Malthouse Press, 1990.

Mowah, U. *Eating By the Flesh*. Ibadan: Kraft Books Ltd., 1995.

Nasiru, A. *Our Survival*. Lagos: Macmillan, 1985.

Nduka, U. *Flower Child*. Lagos: Update Communications Ltd., 1988.

Nduka, U. *The Bremen Poems*. New Leaf Press, 1995.

Nwachukwu-Agbada. *God's Big Toe*. Lagos: Longman, 1987.

Nwosu, M. *The Suns of Kush*. Lagos: Mace Associates Ltd., 1995.

Obafemi, O. *Naira Has No Gender*. Ibadan: Kraft Books, 1993.

Obong, E. *Garden House*. Ibadan: New Horn Press, 1988.

Odozor, L. U. Words of a Bayonet Man. Manuscript, 1992.

Ofeimun, O. *The Poet Lied*. Lagos: Update Communications Ltd., 1989.

Oguibe, O. *A Gathering Fear*. Ibadan: Kraft Book Ltd., 1992.

Ogundipe-Leslie, M. *Sew the Old Days*. Ibadan: Evans Publishers, 1985.

Ohaeto, E. *The Voice of the Night Masquerade*. Ibadan: Kraft Books Ltd., 1996.

Ojaide, T. *Labyrinths of the Delta*. New York: The Greenfield Review Press, 1986.

Ojaide, T. *The Endless Song*. Lagos: Malthouse Press, 1989.

Ojaide, T. *The Blood of Peace & Other Poems*. Oxford: Heinemann, 1991.

Okediran, W. *Rainbows Are For Lovers*. Ibadan: Spectrum Books, 1987.

Okome, O. *Pendants*. Ibadan: Kraft Books Ltd., 1993.

Okoye, I. *Behind the Cloud*. London: Longman, 1982.

Okoye, I. *Men Without Ears*. London: Longman, 1984.

Okpewho, I. *The Last Duty*. London: Longman, 1976.

Okpewho, I. *Tides*. London: Longman, 1993.

Olusunle, T. *Fingermarks*. Ibadan: Kraft Books Ltd., 1996.

Onwueme, T. *A Hen Too Soon. 1983.*

Onwueme, T. *The Desert Encroaches*. Ibadan: Heinemann, 1987.

Onwueme, T. *Legacies*. Ibadan: Heinemann, 1989.

Onwueme, T. *Tell It To Women*. Ibadan: Heinemann, 1995.

Omobowale, E. B. *The Eagle Must Fly & Other Stories*. Ibadan: Evans Brothers, 1993.

Omotoso, K. *The Edifice*. London: Heinemann, 1971.

Omotoso, K. *Just Before Dawn*. Ibadan: Spectrum Books, 1988.

Osofisan, F. *The Chattering and the Song*. Ibadan: Ibadan University Press., 1976.

Osofisan, F. *Once Upon Four Robbers*. Ibadan: BIO Educational Services Ltd., 1980.

Osofisan, F. *Morountodun & Other Plays*. Lagos: Longman Drumbeat, 1982.

Osofisan, F. "The Oriki of a Grasshopper", in *Two One-Act Plays,* Ibadan: New Horn Press, 1986.

Osofisan, F. (Forthcoming). Nkrumah-Ni — Africa-Ni!

Osofisan, S. *Darksongs*. Ibadan: Heinemann, 1991.

Osundare, N. *Songs of the Marketplace*. Ibadan, New Horn Press, 1983.

Osundare, N. *Waiting Laughters*. Lagos & Oxford: Malthouse Press, 1990.

Osundare, N. *Midlife*. Ibadan: Heinemann, 1993.

Otiono, N. *The Night Hides With a Knife*. Ibadan: New Horn Press, 1995.

Oyebode, F. *Naked to Your Softness and Other Dreams*. Birmingham, U.K.: Ijala Press, 1989.

Oyegoke, L. *Cowrie Tears*. Longman Drumbeat, 1982.

Raji, R. *A Harvest of Laughters*. Ibadan: Kraft Books, 1997.

Raji, W. *Rolling Dreams.* Forthcoming

Saro Wiwa, K. *A Forest of Flowers*. Port Harcourt: Saros International Publishers, 1987.

Saro Wiwa, K. *On A Darkling Plain: An Account of the Nigerian Civil War*. Port Harcourt: Saros International Publishers, 1989.

Segun, O. *The Third Dimple*. Ibadan: Heinemann, 1992.

Shehu, E. U. *Questions for Big Brother*. Lagos: Update Communications Ltd., 1988.

Sowande, B. *Farewell to Babylon & Other Plays*. Harlow: Longman, 1979.

Sowande, B. *Tornadoes Full of Dreams*. Lagos and Oxford: Malthouse Press, 1990.

Udechukwu, O. *What the Madman Said*. Bayreuth: Boomerang Press, 1990.

Udeozo, O. *Excursions*. Jos: Fab Anieh Nig. Ltd., 1993.

Udeozo, O. *Stimulus*. Jos: Fab Anieh Nig. Ltd., 1993.

Ugah, A. *Song of the Talakawa*. Braunton & Devon: Merlin Books, 1983.

Ukala, S. *The Slave Wife*. Ibadan: University Press Ltd., 1982.

Ukala, S. *Break a Boil*. Agbor: Oris Press, 1992.

Ushie, J. (1991). *Popular Stand*. Uyo: Rina, Juen Books, 1991.

Ushie, J. *Lamb at the Shrine*. Ibadan: Kraft Books, 1995.

*BEHOLD THE FEAST; BUT WHERE'S THE GUEST?

Our gathering today reminds me of a story I have been eager to share. Long ago in a town beyond the hills there was a man who towered above the rest like the head above the shoulders. As a farmer his barn was eloquent with yams; as a hunter he never returned from the forest without a magnificent game on his shoulders; as a musician his song was honey to the ears of his listeners; as a sculptor he provoked sundry wood into life-like figures. Everyone spoke of this man's exuberant zest for life: he licked sumptuous pots to the bottom and was on first-name basis with the palm wine.

The townsfolk said his eyes were long and far, his ears keen like dawn's breeze. He was seen many times wondering in the forests or brooding, spirit-like, at the top of the rockhills. He foretold seasons of plenty; he warned against spells of famine. He knew the secret of the rain and traced the itinerant caprices of the clouds. His name mounted the saddle of the winds. His deeds lived in proverbs.

Every king courted his company, but integrity kept him at the safest distance from the palace gate. Every king desired to know what bees brewed the honey in his throat, what fire forged the sharpness of his gun; what whetstone endowed his adze with such amazing keeness. Every king wanted his shadow to fall across the palace grounds. But the louder the call, the faster his run. Knowing acutely well that familiarity with power often breeds contempt of the most pernicious type, he held his shield against the seductive arrows of royal summons. Except for one brief season when he lowered his guard and took one brief sup at the royal table and thereafter beat a hasty retreat, no king really knew his first name.

So when he talked, the people listened, the Crown trembled. He looked Truth straight in the eyes and told it without blinking. He amplified the beggar's wail in the town square and brandished the limbs of those trampled to pieces by the royal horse. The king tempted him with kola nuts; the king tempted him with money; the king tempted him with the most seductive princess in town. But the man simply looked the other way. The king sent him a copy of his royal crown. But our man considered his own head too big for a surrogate cap. The king's fear turned into a tiger with lethal claws. Royal guards went on the prowl. And the man escaped in the first light of an appointed day, unknown to any one except the old moon and the cock.

Soon an advancing season announced the coming of the Festival of Light during which the works and achievements of a prominent townsman were laid out for admiration—and even more, for inspiration. This particular year the accomplishments of the man were the ones on proud and dignifying display. The best of his yams, the best of his beans, his most eloquent sculptures, the most mellifluous of his songs, were all spread out in the town square for wondering eyes and admiring minds. Drummers wore out their sticks; dancers demonstrated the graceful energy of their leaps. And just as the opening speech was about to start, the celebrants noticed a magnificent absence. "These are the deeds", the master of ceremony proclaimed, "but where is the doer?"; "this is the feast, but where is the guest?". . .
. . . . .

It is an eloquent testimony to Wole Soyinka's preeminence as a writer and social presence that he is not with us today. That testimony becomes even more eloquent when we realise that this grand celebration of West African letters is being held in his honour even in his absence. We are constrained to ask: what kind of country, what kind of circumstance, throws out such a substantial jewel in his near-twilight years—at a time when a needy nation should be supremely glad to tap from his vast talent, when his mere presence should be a source of monumental inspiration? Behold, therefore, the books; but where is the author?

Of course, pungent as the above question is, it is also rhetorical. For we all know where Soyinka is. As our people say, *"Ajanku kuro ni mo ri nkan firi"* (The elephant is no animal to behold at a meager glance). Soyinka has ensured his presence by being an artist for whom there can be no absolute separation of art and life, of song and singer. He is a writer in whom the past is constantly interrogated by the present, for whom past and present both anticipate and address the future.

This is why in being the kind of artist that he is, Soyinka is also a vital part of our nation's memory. In his works is a crucial historical consciousness which goes beyond mere narrative flashbacks and convoluted novelistic plots. In him we find a complex interplay of narration and re-construction, a mix of mordant prophecy and visionary admonition. These, for instance, are the high points of *A Dance of the Forests*, Soyinka's first major play (and about his most complex to date) and the one he wrote to commemorate the coming of Nigeria's independence. Events and happenings in Nigeria since 1960, including the ones which led to his recent forced exit, have demonstrated that Nigeria has not yet found a cure for her "half child" syndrome; and that, indeed, the country is still nothing better than "a gathering of the tribes".

A prodigiously versatile and mercurial artist that Soyinka is, the stage still remains his marketplace and forum, his sounding board and public tribunal. In this supreme medium of mime and mask, he confronts us with the monster of hypocrisy in *The Trials of Brother Jero* and *Jero's Metamorphosis*, while *The Lion and the Jewel* (about Soyinka's most popular play) presents a wily traditionalism at loggerheads with half-baked modernism. *Kongi's Harvest* served an early warning about the then emerging political dictatorship in Africa, while *To Zia with Love* considers the international dimension of this political virus. Those who want a taste of Soyinka's mordant satirical wit should make friends with the Blackout plays, while those who desire him at his most sombre should pick through the bones and scattered corpses of *Madmen and Specialists*. A triumphant lyricism breathes through the core of *The Bacchae of Euripedes* where a revolutionary bud sprouts in Dionysian ferment, while in the inimitable *Death and the King's Horseman*, the playwright "commits" music even before protagonist Elesin Oba goes on to "commit death". Horseman will remain for many years both the watershed and ultimate in African tragic dramaturgy; a play in which Soyinka progresses from comptence to profundity, a drama which juxtaposes the beauty of form with the disturbing controversy of content.

To many, Soyinka is the essential dramatist; to others he is primarily a poet. But in real professional terms, it is a case of one faculty complementing the other, producing the essentially accomplished artist. As in his drama, Soyinka the poet is also a medium of many masks and voices. In *Idanre and Other Poems* and *A Shuttle in the Crypt*, the mask is rugged, the idiom obscure almost to the point of esotericism. But a greater audience-awareness, a more urgent social commitment later softened the muscular code so that Ogun Abibiman addressed the imperative of Africa's political liberation in a tone and a tenor hardly encountered in Soyinka's earlier poetry. By the time Mandela' Earth arrived, many critics remarked that, at last, the poet had re-connected his idiom with the people's tongue. This "re-grounding" actually began with Unlimited liability Company a powerfully satirical work which took the country by storm in 1983 and before long became the banter of buka joints.

In virtually all these poems, myth complements history: Ogun descends from the mysty tops of ancient rockhills, foraging through the terror of primal forests, matchet in one hand, a keg of palm wine in the other. And when the sky rumbles in the cloudy distances, Sango pilots the thunder into the blacksmith's forge. Between these two gods is the bridge of destruction and construction, of creation and re-creation. Any wonder, then, that the bard enlists the axe-handed one in the battle against apartheid. Whoever still thinks that the gods are too distant to be poets and warriors, let him have a solemn dialogue with Soyinka's pantheon.

Story-teller of the fertile yarn, Soyinka has created narratives which fit into two overlapping categories: the fiction of *The Interpreters* and *Season of Anomy* is only one short imagination away from the "faction" of *The Man Died*, Ake, Isara, and Ibadan. In both categories Soyinka provides a tapestry of events, a configuration of actions, and an astounding variety of human beings who shape the world in the process of being shaped by it. Our writer has a prodigious sense of place, especially what place does to man and matter through the agency of time. For what is a place if not a site once inhabited but which takes on permanent residence in our memory thereafter.

Soyinka belongs in the category of writers who do not only remember but also remind. That is why both he and his works constitute a vital part of our national history. An unequivocal voice in defence of humanity any day, any time, any where, he has created works which urge us to interrogate the limits and latitudes of Power and the attitudes of those who wield it. In him we have what Seamus Heaney the great poet and essayist has called a rare combination of "song and suffering". Hardly any Nigerian writer has suffered more than Soyinka in the cause of freedom and justice. Hardly any has matched his combination of literary and social activism.

Some writers merely bear witness to the monumental happenings of the day; some are content to be clinical chroniclers of epochal junctures. But Soyinka's is the dynamic impulse in active dialogue with our times, a restless, impatient prodigy which hurries history into a vortex of becoming. Dramatist, poet, novelist, autobiographer, film-maker, music-composer and singer, polemicist, Road Safety Marshal, human rights crusader, here is a writer who relentlessly humanises our consciousness, a writer whose wisdom informs our actions.

But as the master of ceremony asked in the story told earlier: "this is a big feast indeed, but where is the Guest?"

*   Opening address at the British Council Exhibition on West African Writers in celebration of Wole Soyinka's 60th birthday, held at the Nigerian Institute of International Affairs, Lagos, June 19, 1995.

*THE LONGEST DAY

November 10, 1995. The news broke while I was on a train journey between Edinburgh and Birmingham. The day before, I had arrived at the University of Edinburgh as a guest speaker at its Institute of African Studies. It was a cold, somewhat ominous day, one on which some large, indescribable burden seemed to be hanging from the sky. The news on every lip, the anxiety in every heart was the confirmation by Nigeria's military ruling council of a death sentence earlier passed on Ken Saro-Wiwa and eight other Ogoni activists. Once again, the world's eyes turned towards Nigeria. Prayers were said, supplications made, passionate pleas were registered from every corner of the globe: "put a halt to Nigeria's cycle of bloodletting; spare the Ogoni Nine!"

It was a cold day, and the heaviness in my heart almost robbed me of a wholesome appreciation of the venerable serenity of Edinburgh and its famous university. The beauty I saw all around me—the city's breathtaking architecture, the autumnal splendour of the woods, the sheer Scottish ruggedness of the ambiance—all contrasted so touchingly with the ugliness emanating from my dear country and its illegitimate seat of power. How could a country keep polluting the world so recklessly, ever so relentlessly, with the incorrigible bestiality of its deeds and misdeeds?

Everywhere I went in Edinburgh, the atmosphere was electrified by the Ken Saro-Wiwa issue. Everyone wanted to know who Ken really was, why he had become such a thorn in the side of Nigeria's ruling junta, what could be done to pressurise the Nigerian rulers into saving his life. *The Scotsman*, Scotland's leading newspaper, was no doubt in the vanguard of the pro-life campaign. After publishing its interview with me on Ken-Wiwa and the general state of affairs in Nigeria, it was considerate enough to publicize its fears about my own safety in a country where another writer's life was so brutally imperiled.[1]

A cold, ominous day November 9 turned out to be. But good, like-minded company thawed some of the chill: Pravina King of the Institute of African Studies, Femi Folorunso, long-known friend, academic, and progressive thinker, and Angus Calder, versatile scholar and consistently humane Africanist, all lifted my spirit and untied my tongue. Coincidentally, and characteristically, the troublesome interplay between African politics and African literary imagination formed the crux of my lecture. And, deservedly, Ken Saro-Wiwa occupied the opening paragraph, instantly followed by a catalogue of other African men and women of ideas subjected to all kinds of dehumanization at home or forced into a most frustrating exile abroad. From Abacha's Nigeria to Arap Moi's Kenya, from Mobutu's Zaire to Eyadema's Togo, Africa remains the graveyard of freedom, a nether world where dreams die fast, and positive vision is a treasonable offense.

How 'free' can the imagination be in an unfree continent, how uncommitted can it afford to be in a place which commits the writer to death? "It has become absolutely, painfully, clear to us in Africa", my talk continued, that the subversion of the democratic ideal invariably precipitates a disruption of the cultural space. Literature, which represents one of the finest manifestations of the soul and collective imagination of a people needs a reasonable amount of space to breathe, to move around, shuffle its metaphors and spread out its tales.

That space hardly exists anywhere in Africa today; hence the writer's almost divine mission to will it into existence, expa its perimeters with his/her voice and pen. This humanist project calls for an essentially answerable imagination, one that is acutely aware of its place and purpose in society, an active, transitive insight committed by conscience, concretized by experience.

These ideals lay at the root of Ken Saro-Wiwa's literary mission, from the sardonically satirical *Prisoner of Jebs* to some of the contemplative stories in *A Forest of Flowers*. Saro-Wiwa was not only a voice of vision of his own time; he was also the voice of vision of his people, a voice of those rendered voiceless and trampled by the Nigerian behemoth. His pen was getting too large, his image too disturbing. He had 'externalized' the Ogoni issue beyond frontiers containable by the Nigerian rulers. His case urgently called the 'final solution'....

But remember: we are still on November 9, the day before. My talk went down well. The Edinburgh audience was gracious and receptive. And very concerned. Reaction time, and questions and comments centered on African literature in general and the unfolding specificity of the Saro-Wiwa tragedy. In the end, the audience formalized its pro-life position, signed a passionate plea to be forwarded to the Nigerian High Commission. The burden of the message: spare Ken Saro-Wiwa and the other Ogoni activists.

Dinner that evening had the Ken-Saro-Wiwa debate high on the menu list. My hosts and I argued back and forth, guessed, speculated, weighed different options. Some of us argued fervently that no country would so flagrantly waste some of its best citizens no matter the temptation to vengeful extremism. Not at the very time the Commonwealth was meeting. Not when some of the world's most respectable leaders, including Nelson Mandela, had entered a plea and drawn some assurance. Not when the Ogoni cause for which the condemned men risked their lives, was so just. Not when... not when... But one of my hosts who seemed to possess an uncanny insight into military dictatorships and their macabre ways, was clearly less sanguine. After Idi Amin and Bokassa, he warned, we should, indeed, be careful about setting an upper limit for military excesses in Nigeria. We parted that evening hoping that his fears would turn out to be helpfully unjustified.

November 10. The morning was crisp and urgent. The sun bounced off the roofs and dazzled the streets with a brightness unusual in that period of the year. My eyes threaded the sky for signs and intimations. None immediately suggested itself to me. My mind flashed back to my dear country, Nigeria, and to Ken Saro-Wiwa. I imagined that feisty spirit on death row, and wondered what must be going through his fecund mind. My hosts, Pravin King and Femi Folorunso, broke into my reverie. "Time to hurry off to the railway station now; your train is due in another hour." "Any news about my dear country?" I asked, my lips quaking with anxiety. "No news. Just a catalogue of appeals, appeals, appeals." "I'm sure those appeals will work", I reasoned, "no government can turn a deaf ear to this uproar from all the corners of the globe." "I'm more fearful than hopeful in this particular case", Femi cautioned.

The train arrived with a typical British promptitude. I said farewell to my friends, and in a few seconds I was Birmingham-bound. The smoothness of the tracks did nothing to relieve the jauntiness of my mind. "Will Nigeria really murder Ken and eight others? Will my country perpetuate its cycle of waste and stupidity? Will it? Will it not?" My mind broke into two chambers, one full of fear, the other inhabited by faith. I tried to kill my anxiety by wrestling with some of the short-listed entries for the year's BBC Africa Performance competition for which I was judge. Only a brief relief rewarded by effort. Somewhat I remembered Ikemefuna on that last and fateful journey, his wish for life so different, so distant from the machinations of those blood-thirsty warlords behind him, their sharpened machetes itching in their scabbards. But will Nigeria kill Ken and eight others? Will it? Will it not?

Birmingham at last, and back to my place of temporary abode. A slight push on the bell, and my hostess was at the door, her face heavy with unspoken grief. "They have been hanged", she said, "the radio announced it a while ago." My bag dropped from my hands. My tongue tasted like a lump of acid. I collapsed on the lower steps of the stairs, my head jammed by unspeakable thoughts. "Why don't you move over to the dining table?" my hostess implored, "Dinner is ready, and there is a Ghanian friend I've brought to meet you before your return to Nigeria. I complied, shook hands with my Ghanaian colleague, and grief-stricken, we exchanged sad notes about Africa and her bloody woes. Dinner being absolutely uneatable, I staggered upstairs and into bed.

No sleep came within a thousand kilometres of my bed that night. No sleep. Only milling memories which reinforced my frightening sense of loss. I remembered the short, ebullient Ken, his patented pipe in his mouth, his riveting sense of humor, his wit and swagger, his mischievous sense of drama, his gargantuan ambitiousness which came in inverse proportion to his small physical frame. In particular, I remembered one of Ken's last public lectures in Ibadan. The irrepressible guest speaker had mounted the podium, scaled the microphone down to his height, then asked the audience (in humorous mockery of his minuscule stature):can you see me?

This was the style of the man who rattled us into wakefulness and would not allow our social conscience a single moment of complacency. Whether it is the jibes of *Prisoner of Jebs*, the near-Augustan excoriation of Pita Dumbrock, the cash-and-carry satire of *Basi and Company*, the cry-as-you-laugh yarn of *Soza Boy*, or the clamorously partisan narrative of *On a Darkling Plain*, Saro-Wiwa, poet, novelist, dramatist, journalist, polemicist, publisher, human rights activist..., left an indelible imprint on Nigerian letters and the Nigerian spirit. His commitment was total, his vision complex but staunchly humane. Can it really be true that this multi-talented life has been wasted in my dear country Nigeria? Won't the radio come on again and tell the world that the previous report was a lie, some Nigerian functionary has been misquoted, as usual? Won't someone say that Ken has not been killed?

The following day's newspaper ridiculed my wishful thinking with gory details of Saro-Wiwa's hanging. And for several days after, British newspapers concentrated on Nigeria with ferocious intensity. Even the usually conservative Times came out with an editorial roundly condemning Nigeria's foul dictatorship. Several articles and letters to the editor literally cursed Nigerian rulers for inflicting such untold barbarism on our common humanity. It was a difficult time to be a Nigerian; many became vicarious victims of Nigerian rulers' crimes. And over to Auckland, New Zealand, Commonwealth leaders received the news with palpable shock and anguish, many of them calling for reprisals. John Major, British Prime Minister, called the hanging "judicial murder." He, too, supported reprisals but I knew things would change with time, given the cunning duplicity that has always characterised British dealings with Nigeria.

My brief sojourn in Britain over, I stepped into the plane, bound for Nigeria, the country which wastes us so brutally, but which remains so steadfast in the center of our dreams. Upon arrival, my first point of contact were my Association of Nigerian Authors (ANA) compatriots, Ken's other family which he once led with indefatigable commitment, and whose annual convention was in full progress when news of his hanging froze the world. In particular, I wanted to know how the abomination was received by Stewart Brown, a highly sensitive and humane British scholar and writer who was my chief host in Birmingham before coming over to Nigeria as the convention's guest speaker. The pain was deep and cruel. Responses came in clipped clauses and seething grimace. Under it all I sensed, no, felt, a stirring undercurrent of eloquence and anger. I beheld a Ken Saro-Wiwa living forever in our songs and fable while his murderers

> ...sure fade into history
> Remembered only when tales are told
> Of midday dreams
> And spectres on the market day.[2]

*   An essay marking the first anniversary of Ken Saro-Wiwa's hanging.

Notes

1. *The Scotsman*. Friday, November 10, 1995, p. 11.
2. Niyi Osundare, 'To the Dinosaur', *Songs of the Marketplace*. Ibadan: New Horn Press, 1983, p. 42.

*THE TRAVAILS OF EFFICIENCY

"The Future belongs to the efficient", proclaimed the advertisment slogan of one of the public utility companies in the United States in the seventies. At first I used to classify this highly declarative assertion as part of the usual American "big talk" syndrome. For is it not the case that that part of the globe is the home of superlatives, a place where the word "best" is used so often that you would think that its humbler root "good" had simply disappeared from the dictionary, a place where to be really media-worthy you have to progress from the status of a mere star to that of a super star, then megastar, and later mega mega star? America is a land of hyperboles where humility sometimes looks like one of the cardinal sins, and simple modesty is a sure invitation to social suicide.

However, there is some beauty in the American boast: behind each bloated claim is a dream; behind each dream is a commitment and idealism frequently total and aggressive (the rest of the world may not always agree with this dream, but that is a different matter). In some respects the deliberate hyperbole in American discourse may be seen as a prior psychological commitment to the dictates and demands of its proclamations, a verbal and rhetorical pledge which insists upon future fulfilment.

American "big talk" is not just an elaborate massage of the national ego; it is a sure booster of that ego, a desideratum for its health and sustenance. In other words, America talks big because it can also act big. Put another way, America talks big so as to be able to act big. Much of what is called the "American Dream" is therefore locatable in the people's words and phrases. Quite often, wishful thinking, if properly managed, may result in wish fulfilment.

A nation that wants to grow must know how to dream, how to anticipate, how to fore-see, how to fore-plan. It must not be scared of building castles in the air if that would guarantee putting them on the ground eventually. (After all if no one built castles in the air there would be no architects!) It must constantly seek ways of bettering its good and besting its better. This is the open secret of those parts of the world we now routinely describe as developed. Their enviable status is hinged on the attainment of efficiency, that great virtue without which dreams for ever remain dreams, while progress stays mired in flightless stupor.

Now, efficiency is not just a way of doing things. It is a means and a method achieved through systematic training and constant practice. In operational terms, whether human or mechanical, it is that capacity to act or produce proficiently with minimum waste and cost, and without unnecessary effort, so that in the end the quality of output is justifiable to the standard of input. Efficiency is no par with mere skillfulness. It ranks higher than competence on the ladder of human capability. At its most ideal, efficiency progresses from rigor to habit, works itself into the personal and national psyche, and occupies a prominent niche in thc national grid of values. At that point a quality code enters the national lexicon, with maxims of discernment and positive discrimination. What was fabulously satisfying in a previous age becomes merely tolerable with advanced judgement. Erstwhile formidable frontiers are pushed forward with new methods. The moonland of previously wild imaginations becomes a concrete space on which human feet actually leave unforgettable imprints. Between science and efficiency is a marvelous mutual determination and dependency. And it is to the former two that modernity and civilization owe their inevitably.

The future does not only belong to the efficient; the past also did. Come to think of it: Africa has always been the victim of the ruthlessness of other people's efficiency. Several decades before slave ships set sail for the Black continent there were the "voyages of discovery". Before those voyages there were centuries of astronomical speculations and sundry projections about the geography of the universe: its seas, oceans, and rivers; the lands and peoples beyond those waters. Without courage, without knowledge and the relative mechanical efficiency produced by that knowledge, without a sense of adventure (and, of course, the overweening zeal to conquer and grab for king/queen and country), the early European adventurers would hardly have been able to venture beyond their shores, talk less of gaining the chance to plunder Africa for their respective countries.

Think about the turbulent seas, more mysterious, more awesome in those days. Think about rickety ships so easily capsized by angry waters. Think about scurvy, malaria and other death-haulers which made short work of many a crew. But the white men kept coming, perfecting their navigational skills every voyage, discovering new medication to shore up their immunity, until they were able to bring large ships which left African shores with enormous human cargo. This lasted many years and Africa lost the cream of its human stock. When the industrial revolution produced its own kind of efficiency which changed modes of labor and made the slave trade uncost-effective, this new efficiency shifted attention to the exploitation of Africa's natural and mineral resources. Africa's cocoa, coffee, tea, cotton, rubber, timber, etc. poured into progressively efficient European and American factories. Europe grew richer, Africa poorer. Add to all this the savagely efficient gunboats and canon which drowned African resistance in blood, making European conquest so demonically easy.

All these are the foster parents of the present neo-colonial condition (some people delight in misrepresenting this condition by calling it "post-colonial"!). Today technological efficiency and calculated socioeconomic agenda have kept Europe and America very much in the center, and firmly in control; the West manufactures, Africa consumes; the IMF dictates economic blueprints and plants its police in the central bank of virtually every African country. The naira has no value except in relation to the dollar or the pound. Today what economists call the IPC (Income Per Capita) has been replaced by DPC (Debt Per Capita). Each African owes the money houses of the industrial world enough debt to last three or four generations—thanks to the murderous robbers and stone-age tyrants under whose rulership Africa keeps tottering like a rudderless ship.

Efficiency. That ability to make the world work for maximum output with minimum input, that ability to master the forces of the universe to maximum human advantage, that facility for controlling nature, the environment (without devastating them), that genius for probing the mystery of the unknown, for anticipating the future and making preparations for its baffling contingencies —these are golden virtues so crucially scarce in Nigeria. This explains why one of the world's most endowed countries stubbornly remains one of its poorest, most disorganised, most barbaric. It takes a modicum of action, of efficiency, to convert inertia into motion, then movement. A country may sit on one of the largest iron ore deposits in the world and yet till the land with sticks and fight wild animals with crude clubs. A country may be literally drowning in crude petroleum and yet suffer fuel shortages on a regular basis. It is the basic law of nature that many things do not move unless they are moved—or pushed. For the movement to satisfy the original intent, it must be backed up—indeed inaugurated—by a unit of intelligence. The more refined that intelligence, and the higher its efficiency quotient, the smoother the movement, the more satisfactory the result is likely to be.

Efficiency is therefore not just another attainment resulting from educational crash programs or hasty workshops on national planning. Its essence is too subtle, too precious for the calligraphic trumpet of boastful certificates. Efficiency is not just a way of doing; it is also a doing potential, a can-do. It is epistemological and sociological, personal and social. After a long period of operational existence, it becomes a cultural practice.

Despite the hollow noise of budget speeches and ritual posturing of public functionaries, Nigeria has really never extolled the culture of efficiency. We are a country too ready to deal on the surface, too willing to sweep problematic truth under the carpet. A country where people are too scared—or too opportunistic—to ask questions, and insist on answers. We are too readily satisfied with too little, too easily bribed with specious argumentation. We are people who mistake the sounding for the meaning, who read so rapidly on the lines, hardly between the lines. In this country the quality of achievement is measured by the number of houses owned, the quantity and variety of cars in the driveway, the prodigal finery in the wardrobe, etc. Externalities. Pageantry. Spectacle. A people so taken up by the tinsel glow of the shell can hardly think their way to the nut beyond the crust.

Which is why we are a people of quick-fix solutions, placebos, and fast-food-for-thought. Shamans and charlattans thrive so blissfully in this land. False prophets and millionaire messiahs clog our faith-channels with deadening forecasts and apocryphal visions. Bombarding us with the Edenic illusions of their apocalyptic imaginations, they sabotage our will and the ability to come to grips with the realities of this sorely abused country and the monsters that have made our existence so miserable and brutish. When every ruler no matter how murderous, how tyrannical, is so dogmatically proclaimed "God-sent", aren't we back to the bank of the Red Sea with Pharaoh's cavalry in hot pursuit - but with neither Moses nor his wand in sight?

Our national thought lacks the necessary measure of efficiency. Which is why our national discourse stands in need of rigor: the capacity to turn facts over several times before assaying an opinion, the capacity to question, to argue, to look platitudes in the face and force them to blink and vanish. Shoddiness and its rubbishy relations take us hostage as a people because we are not efficient enough to insist on the best. Quite often we seek refuge under slavish adaptability. When electricity fails, as it frequently does, we change the grid to gas; when gas runs out (in a country with one of the largest gas deposits on earth), we pull out the kerosine stove; when that too, dries up we pick up our matchets and head for the bush for firewood; if firewood is not available, we go in search of saw dust.... In the same vein when water supply fails, we try to "solve" the problem by littering the landscape with private wells and boreholes. We turn the other cheek too readily. We are a people too easy to take for granted. The reason public utilities are so scandalously inefficient in Nigeria is due largely to the inefficiency in the public accountability system. This same reason is responsible for the impunity with which public functionaries loot the country's treasury and abuse its trust. The inefficient system also makes crime detection difficult and punishment impossible. In places with more accountable traditions, citizens know their rights, taxpayers their dues. And more important, they know how to insist on them!

In Nigeria we build the bridge before looking for the river. We plant the cart solidly before the horse and then wonder why we are not "moving forward". Hardly do we think about loose ends and blind spots; hardly do we ruminate about vital "if's" and "just-in-case's". That imaginative amplitude, that predictive capability without which all projections are dead ends, are scarcely the virtues of those whose duty it is to reason this country into the next millennium. Our visual field is too narrow; our sky is just a few meters above the roof. This is why the country keeps hobbling like a goat whose hind legs are tied. Let me illustrate these assertions with a simple anecdote.

There is a road in one of our large cities, which for several years was the terror for all motorists. Its potholes were large and deep enough to swallow up a Bedford lorry; and when it rained, its clogged gutters spewed abominable mess all over its surface. Motorists mumbled and cursed as they plodded along this road, some of them taking out their anger on their equally afflicted fellow road-users. But nobody's focus was efficient enough to zero in on the government ministry whose dereliction had led to the wreck of so many cars and so many purses. No one dared to think about calling the governor's attentions to this death trap that was one of the major roads in his state capital. The road deteriorated every passing week until one of its culverts snapped, cutting a major street into two impassable strips.

It remained that way until a state commissioner discovered it and decided to do something. After many weeks of painstaking labor, the road's rehabilitation was complete. Motorists pumped their horns as their wheels glided along. Pedestrian soles rejoiced at the touch of fresh tar. But that joy was short-lived. Exactly five days after the graders and caterpillars had left, about half a dozen men came with pick axes and shovels and dug a wide hole across the road. Their mission? To restore a water pipe! When asked why they had chosen that time, of all times, for their assignment, their answer was disarmingly simple: the ministry of works and transport has its schedule, the water department has its own; and one schedule cannot stand in the way of the other. And these were two organs of the same government! Is anyone asking questions about planning and coordination, about foresight? Is government really concerned about that beast called efficiency? The hole dug by the water people became the vulnerable spot in the new road. The next season's rains crept in through there and got under the tarred layer. Soon, a battery of potholes appeared again, and a once beautiful road reverted to a ragged mess.

Why are we so hasty, so shoddy in our doings? Why are we so scared of thinking? How so readily we concede original thought and inventiveness to other people while we remain so blissfully contented with faint echoes and ventriloqual murmurs! I have never ceased to wonder why some Nigerians would rather be "manufacturers' representatives" than choose to be manufacturers themselves, why people would rather invest their capital in the importation of second-hand clothes from overseas than establish a textile factory in Nigeria. But I see at the root of it all a combination of improvidence and the craving for instant gratification. Establishing an industry and nurturing it into profitable maturity demand much more patience and vision - much more efficiency - than knocking up a trading post. Nigeria has never been a country of long-term projections and systematic implementation, but those who want to run modern institutions on venal medieval passions should learn a thing or two from the catastrophic crash of the flashy banks and finance houses which mushroomed in the so-called Babangida years.

This is not to say that Nigerian rulers are completely ignorant of the virtues of efficiency and the technological wonders that are its inalienable companion. But their dreamt-up route to these wonders is almost invariably naive, laughably inefficient. Time there was when the government policy was to technologize the country tipa tipa (by force), when public functionaries boasted that the country was ready to "buy, borrow, and/or steal" technology in order to join other nation states in the race for the future. A very perverse ambition it has all turned out to be, itself a sour product of inefficient thinking. About two decades later, it has now dawned on us that: technology is not a salable commodity (the petro dollars of the willing buyer notwithstanding); technology is not a neighbor's hoe that can be borrowed and returned after use ("owners of technology" do not play Father Christmas with their knowledge); technology cannot be stolen (those owners have an efficient method for securing their prized possession). Not even the present pretence which leads us into branding cars assembled in our foreign-dominated factories as MADE IN NIGERIA will bring our technological dream to fruition.

For technology is the legitimate offspring of a home-grown efficiency. It requires the right climate, the appropriate soil chemistry, an enabling culture. A sound educational system is a vital part of that culture. Is any one still asking how efficient our educational system is today? With Stone Age laboratories and outdated libraries how can we nurture those minds that will create home-grown technology without having to buy or borrow or steal? How educationally efficient can students grow to be when they spend nine months of the year out of school due to one national crisis or another? What about malnourished babies of malnourished mothers, whose mental faculties are already incapacitated by an inadequate intake of protein and other vital nutrients? How efficient can the Nigerian university professor be when his/her entire take-home salary is less than the entertainment allowance of a bank manager? What prospects for intellectual break-through in a country which ridicules original thinking, terrorises creative dissent, and pays lip service to positive inventiveness? In brief, how can an inefficient arrangement produce efficient results?

Weighty questions indeed, but let me begin my home call. In a recent inaugural lecture at the University of Ibadan, my colleague Professor Doyin Soyibo articulated a lively affiliation between "the power of ideas" and "the idea of power". Those who hold the reins in Nigeria have always embraced "power" without the transformative potency of positive "ideas". But power without efficiency can only end up brutish and misdirected, a kind of saber rattling in a medieval jungle. The real power of ideas, the essence of efficiency reside in the old unassailable values of industry, thoroughness, and assiduity; a gigantic appetite for knowledge, unflinching tenacity, a meticulous, almost finicky attention to little details, precision, the gift of foresight and fore-planning. Nobody, no country, can get to the top - and stay there for long - without these virtues.

The 21st century is a mere four years away. Will Nigeria stumble into it with an inefficient political arrangement which frustrates genuine democracy and fosters Stone Age dictatorship in a world that is becoming more and more intolerant of despotism of whatever complexion? Shall we embarrass that century with the same antediluvian communication system, decrepit infrastructures and sundry incoherences that have hobbled our march in the past hundred years? More specifically, will Nigeria and its NEPA(National Electric Power Authority) have mastered the generation of electricity (now considered routine and taken for granted in saner parts of the world) so that we do not have, again, to grope in darkness through that century? How can we prevent the 21st century from being another wasted apoch?

*   Paper delivered at the installation of Dr. Tubosun Adefolaju as the 36th Presi-dent of the Rotary Club of Ibadan on July 4, 1996.

*IBADAN:
IMAGES IN RUST AND GOLD

Take a trip to Mapo Hill one auspicious evening. Take a walk round Mapo Hall, allowing your eyes to soak up every hint, every detail of this titanic building. Fancy the astounding solidity of its Romanesque arches and columns, its tall masculine pillars, its teasingly baroque ambiance. Consider the countless storms and winds weathered yearly by the pale-yellow courage of the walls. Move closer to those walls: dare them. Scratch one of them. What bursts through to your ears is a laughter concrete with history: memories of the robust spirit which forded through the forests of the beginning; memories of those whose virgin steps unclothed the hills; vibrations of their panting breaths; memories of the khaki-trousered, helmet-headed colonial administrator insisting, like a stern headmaster, on "labour" and "service"; memories of the confounding plan in his pocket; memories of the "natives" who laid the stones slab by slab till a historic structure erupted from their hands, standing so imposingly, so strangely on Mapo's hill of hills. Memories, above all, of dreams dreamt on sweltering nights finding eloquent fulfillment on the bed of intriguing dawns. Memories, still, of the resonances of those dreams.

Continue your journey. Past that gate which leads to the octagonal awe of Olubadan's new palace, past the Mapo police station and its running cauldron of charges and bails; past the FM station of the Broadcasting Corporation of Oyo State (BCOS) where air waves are laden with polyglot vibrations. Stand on the many -stepped terrace in the steep apron of the Mapo edifice, give your eyes the generous sweep of the zoom lens of a voracious camera. Then think of what you see.

Facing you directly is the famous Orita Merin and beyond; to your right is Beere, to your left is that road which hurries through countless districts to join the "Lagos Bye-Pass" at Molete; behind you, beyond Mapo Hall, is another intermesh of districts and neighborhoods whose names belong to a memory beyond recall.

Or take a ride in a low-flying plane. Drop your eyes through its oval windows. From your humble height, ponder the hundreds, thousands, millions of houses resting eaves-to-eaves interspersed by tortuous, unsure roads looking like black serpents. Increase your altitude, widen your angle of vision, and what catches the eye is a canvas of colors, principally brown, edged round by a ring of green in urban outskirts where trees and flowers in centrifugal flight eke out a (brief) respite. From whatever angle you look at Ibadan, from whatever perspective, on whatever day of the year, what invariably meets your gaze is a city thronged, complex, and relentlessly plural.

Part of this complexity is the city's handling of the phenomena of tradition and modernity. These two states are themselves very difficult to manage: at times they manifest in harmonious fusion; at times they tolerate each other in uneasy juxtaposition; while at other times they stand, daggers drawn, on either side of an infuriating divide. Complementing this gulf and at times complicating it, is the town-country continuum. Many times, one is at pains to fathom whether Ibadan is a village which became a city, or a city in the process of becoming a village. Squat, windowless houses rub shoulders with futuristic skyscrapers (more on this later); big-domed mosques cast a careful eye on high-spired churches, while both share adherents with shrines where people still bow to native deities whose names the worshipers really know; jazz and punk rock share air waves with sakara and tatolo; while the breakfast tray may have eko agidi and akara sitting next to bread, bacon and egg. Not long ago, I spotted the ancient Oloolu masquerade in plastic shoes; one of his acolytes ran, whip in hand, in a three-piece European suit.

This is why in 1962 when I saw Mapo Hall for the first time as a member of an excursion group from Amoye Grammar School, Ikere-Ekiti, what tickled my araoke (country boy's) imagination was what that foreign structure could be doing on the revered crest of a great African city. (Before then my only encounter with such structures had been in Roman films). I thought Mapo Hall would welcome us with a Latin phrase. It didn't. On the contrary it flowered out in that slow-paced, laid-back highly picturesque dialect of the City-of-Seven-Hills. Mapo Hall is the meeting of two cultures, one European, the other African, both ancient, but trying to find a fertile accommodation with restless modernity. Any wonder then that this brief celebration of Ibadan should start from Mapo Hill, a place....

Places. Places make people, people places. Places have their own names in the register of human memory, in the diary of human experience. A road with a peculiar bend, a street with a file of queer alleys, a river whose singular feature is its leisurely lilt, forests with a memorable fragrance, hills like breasts of magic maidens, markets, parks, schools, spots where heroes were buried, spot where a notorious tyrant was hanged. Places and their names, names and their places.

A place is not the sum total of footprints left in its streets, not just roads, tracks, alleyways made familiar by frequent treading. A place is not just a battery of doors swinging on calibrated hinges, nor a fair of windows which let in the season's winds. A place is all this—and more; the tree which remembers its root, the arrow which knows its quiver, the drum which anticipates the sound of the skin of a fleeing game; eyes which smell; noses which see the trail of familiar districts. What is a city if not itself a place.

Ibadan is a place made up of other places. Hence its intriguing plurality; hence its protean complexion. Take Yemetu, Popo Yeosa, Idi Arere, Elekuro, Ayeye, Beere etc. with their rusty roofs and low mud walls crowded, jostling for space like crabs at the bottom of a bucket, yet so indigenous, so vibrant. Compare with those other places: Oke, Bola, Oke Ado, Odo Ona, Apataganga, Orogun, which used to be urban outskirts but are rapidly being pushed to the urban core. Match these two groups of places with Iyaganku, Jericho, Bodija, Orita Bashorun, Owode where the upper class and upwardly mobile class plant their homes far from the city's madding crowd. Here streets are paved and wide; water supply hardly fails, population density is low, and there is a car in every drive way. So when you talk about Ibadan, which place do you really mean?

Is it the busy skyline of Dugbe, the commercial heart of Ibadan where Cocoa House, recently rehabilitated after a most brutal fire, stands, the 25 stories of it, a shining monument to those bygone days when the farmer was king and cocoa was truly the tree of money? I remember the story my father brought back to Ikere the first time he saw this ile awosifila (the house you look up at and the cap falls off your head). His tale about it all looked so tall to us that it instantly became part of our oral lore. I also remember my old man saying in a typically humorous, ironic way that everyone he saw at that "Ile Awon agbe" (Farmers' House) was either in coat and tie or in a silk dress and high-heeled shoes. The first day I encountered Cocoa House myself, the old myths evaporated, and the contradictions deftly pointed out earlier on by my father stared me straight in the face.

For long, then, Cocoa House was the supreme commander of Ibadan heights, visible from virtually every corner of the city's undulating terrain. It was an excursion site, a towering Mecca for all pilgrims lured hence by their faith in the potency of modern architectural magic.

Cocoa House monopolised the sky until the dramatic entry of Broking House, brainchild and property of Femi Johnson, visionary businessman and versatile artist who planted his own structure a scant hundred yards from the domain of its older rival. Broking House is not only newer, it is more modern, more futuristic with its lavish glass walls which mirror the grace and grass in its uneven surroundings; with its illuminated letters which spell its owner's name with distinctively yellow eloquence, especially on dark nights. Johnson's tall poetry of glass and steel has bequeathed an array of like structures. In an era of banking boom, banks and financial houses are joining in the race for the skyward extension of a predominantly sprawling city.

In other areas modernity seems to be gaining the upper hand. The throbbing markets of Dugbe and Gbagi have been relocated to the outskirts of the city, several miles from their former sites. This change of place is accompanied by a significant change of mode. The open market system of the former venues is yielding place to the "lock-up stall" transactions of the new. Government may boost its revenues from this new arrangement, but the open poetry of the indigenous market may well be the regrettable victim. For, tell me, who can chant hawking ditties in lock-up stalls?

Places. More places. Another port of call, the University of Ibadan, the oldest university in Nigeria, and, no doubt, the most prestigious. Alma Mater of Soyinka, Africa's first Nobel Laureate in Literature, of Achebe, Ade Ajayi, Mabel Segun, Bola Ige, Bolanle Awe, Omolayole, Higo, Ifeajuna, Ciroma, and thousands of other men and women in various fields and trades who passed through the university when its population was a few hundreds and must be delightfully surprised to see the over 25,000 students who throng in their footsteps today. Many still talk nostalgically of those UCI (University College, Ibadan) days when they spoke real Queen's English, sat at dinner table in academic gown and mortar board, and relished the best meals that any country could offer the delicate palate of a burgeoning elite. At this time, Ibadan University was a gown virtually far from its adjoining town: boarding a UCI-bound bus from Dugbe was like preparing for an elaborate out-of-town journey. Undergraduates then were rare, next to gods on earth. Alumni coming back now must wonder what town and gown have done to the distance between them: the university has not only merged with the tempo of the city; at the moment an uneasy high-density village, Agbowo, sprawls only a stone throw from the university gates. But the UAC-built Trenchard Hall is still there, noted more for festive parties now than for nervous examinations; the Tower Clock is still visible around the campus, though its hands are frequently like Maradona's "hand of God", either too fast or too slow for human comprehension.

Places. More places. Another set of gowns, a related set of dreams. A few kilometres from Ibadan University, on the same side of Oyo Road lies the International Institute of Tropical Agriculture (IITA), a center which, true to its name, ministers to the interests of scholars and researchers from numerous parts of the world. The first experience of the visitor is the imaginative topography of the IITA. Some natural denizens of this landscape are left in their useful wildness, the tamed ones are handled in a manner which retains a little bit of their original flavor. Thus in the main what we have here is a certain tampering with nature without completely upsetting its equilibrium.

But the IITA is not designed to be just an exercise in landscape and horticulture; its primary objective is the propagation of a science which puts hunger to flight through the production of food crops that yield better and faster. Its experimental farms attest eloquently to this crusade. Here all kinds of graftings and cross-breedings command attention, and some yields are so big, so unusual that they look veritably magical to the visiting eye.

The IITA is also a place unlike other places in Ibadan. Look right as you enter through its main drive, and you instantly think you are in Florida in the United States, stand on the bridge at the foot of the lake and cast your gaze across the water, and you will be right to swear that you are in a European countryside. There is order here, there is harmony, there is a certain tranquility which gives the IITA the image of a place apart, where discipline is strict (some say severe), and lethargy is not condoned. Each time I visit the IITA I come away with mixed feelings: happy that at least this kind of place is possible in Nigeria, sad that it is possible at the moment largely because the institute is mainly under foreign control. The IITA, then, is both an indictment and a possibility. It is not just a place; it is a parable.

And talking about places and parables, can there be a more suitable juncture to reminisce about those spots which once functioned as Ibadan City's house of dreams? The old British Council center, for example, where, in addition to coming in contact with the best in English literature and language, I also had the opportunity to see many art exhibitions and listen to various talks and readings. Or the legendary Mbari Centre where the ingenious Ulli Beier midwifed some of the most profound artistic talents in Africa. Here it was that I met (no, 'saw' will be a better word!) the prodigious Wole Soyinka for the first time in the sixties. A bearded ample-maned, tempestuous, relentlessly creative young man, Soyinka was a sight to behold, an inspiration to ponder. His voice was so rich and vibrant that even if he could not carry me along with his metaphors, he did so with the magic of their sounding. So iconoclastic, so creatively different was this man in his Okene-cloth danshiki that he just couldn't help becoming a role model for many people of my age who experienced his aura.

There was also Christopher Okigbo, patron-saint of modern Nigerian poetry, who enjoyed writing poetry as much as he cherished the softnesses of life. I was more overwhelmed by the music of his poetry than its meaning. J. P. Clark came closest to writing the kind of poetry fairly within our comprehension. His images were rich and homely, imbued with an Achebe-like simplicity. But Clark's poetry was accessible in a way the poet himself was not. He was distant most of the time. There was also Demas Nwoko, a gifted artist whose verbal eloquence was no match for that of his paint brush. He was closest to Soyinka in mode of dressing and quite a sight too. Wale Ogunyemi, Tunji Oyelana were then buds about to bloom. I remember in particular Ogunyemi's supple versatility and Oyelana's dark-spectacled virtuosity.

This was a time to dream, a time to grow. Unfortunately about a decade later, the British Council left, and artistic activities ceased at Mbari.[1] The Nigerian civil war claimed Okigbo's life, and General Gowon put Soyinka behind bars. Soon after, these centers of artistic excellence became nests without birds. Ibadan city has not regained this artistic tempo ever since, despite current efforts at Bode Sowande's Odu Themes Meridian and the creative renaissance at Kave Klub (founded and administered by the multi-talented architect, Kunle Bolarinwa).

In the past three decades or so, Ibadan city has passed through a series of transformations and metamorphoses. Like the rest of Nigeria, the city too has gone from the plenitude of the oil boom to the bewildering austerity of the years after. One of the most obvious signs of the boom was the vivacity of Ibadan markets, in particular, the astounding variety of commercial goods at Dugbe, Gbagi, and Lebanon Street. Roadside markets sprang up everywhere, spotting textiles and electronic gadgets from virtually every corner of the globe.

Nightlife was vigorous, rich, and joyously noisy. New night clubs sprang up on every street (there was a time I could count three of them in the stretch between the Sango junction and the Polytechnic, a distance of about one quarter kilometre). While old chestnuts like The Seven Sisters (near Liberty Stadium) could not resurrect with the booming seventies, veterans like Grandstand (Oremeji) witnessed an increase of activity, while others spruced up themselves, purchased "heavy" instruments in consonance with the gbi-gbi gban-gban dictates of the disco tradition. A disco "joint" called Harmony erupted on the top floor of a three-storey building on Polytechnic Road; another one, Yesmina, conquered Lebanon Street with its sonic vibrations. But without doubt, the commanding heights of the disco epic in the mid-seventies were at Chrisbo Gardens, Odo Ona where a refurbished mansion attracted nightbirds, and an enlarged, dark-lit dancing floor kept enthusiastic crowds gyrating from dusk to dawn.

This, to many people, was Nigeria's finest hour: an oil-fueled economy bubbled like a water balloon; the naira was strong and proud. Money flowed, and so did beer and oblivious orgies. Ibadan city had her own share of Nigeria's festive seasons. Nightlife was relatively safe and free. Ibadan University students used to walk back to the campus from Dugbe or Mokola at 3 o'clock in the morning at a time when, except for the aerodrome, the entire stretch from Sango to U. I. was a thick and awesome forest! There were strident alarms about armed robbery in many parts of the country, but Ibadan remained ostensibly immune, intriguingly quiet. That is, until its own bubble burst, and the season's musketeers entered the city with bullets in their handshake.

Places. People(s). Transformations. Walking through haunts and joints in Ibadan city so friendly, so familiar in the seventies,

I am forcibly drawn to things that have been. Some places have taken on new names. In some instances both name and "place" are gone, only their memory remains. Take, once again, the British Council Building at Dugbe, an erstwhile artistic center now hemmed in by giant banks. Or the famed Mbari, squatting anonymously now in a row of poverty-afflicted shacks. Would Soyinka still cast a look as he drives by his former Adamasingba roost? What would Okigbo say if he should suddenly rise from the grave today? How many times would Ulli Beier shake his head?[1]

Still other transformations. Who could have believed two decades ago that where the earthy Paradise Hotel used to stand would now be the proud host to Femi Johnson's futuristic Broking House? Hotels and nightlife generally seem to be vulnerable pawns in the entire chess of historical change. Metro Hotel, first to the left as one turns from Lagos Byepass to Ososami Road, has now become something of a flower depot. And yet it was at this spot I first met Idowu Animashaun, Prince Adekunle, Captain Jide Ojo, and other night-riders of the seventies. Ekotedo, a famous red-light district dotted with brothels which insisted on being called hotels, has also shaped up to the compulsive puritanism of recent times. The building housing one of its most frequented hotels in those days was recently converted into a hospital!

Further transformations. WNBS/TV[2] which prides itself on being "First in Africa", proceeded from its status as the exclusive property of the Western State to being one of many stations in a national network. Its state-owned, UHF stablemate, TSOS[3], arrived in 1983, becoming BCOS[4] after integrating its radio and television services a couple of years later. Even Radio Nigeria, for the most curious reason, changed from the handier, neater NBC[5] to FRCN[6]. Whatever new names they decide to bear, whatever areas of operation they elect to pursue, one fact is certain: these broadcasting stations have enriched social and cultural life in Ibadan (and the entire state) in an immeasurable way through their ingenuity in pressing largely foreign mass-media technology into the service of a mainly indigenous audience, within their limits as government-owned organisations. With five different broadcasting channels[7] in its expansive domain, Ibadan occupies a status that many African cities would envy today.

Ibadan, that crowded collage of streets without shoulders, roads with a thousand orita (crossroads), the town-planner's nightmare, but also a roomy haven with a seat for every comer, an accommodating story in a lore of contending tongues. What metaphor can adequately capture the city's many-toned complexion, the nuanced cadence of its accent? From the robust ribaldry of Okebadan festivals to the pious pontifications of mosques and churches, from the lofty majesty of the hills to the watery wrath of Ogunpa, from the exquisite layout of Bodija to the boisterous labyrinth of Popo Yeosa, Ibadan lives every day in bewildering contradictions.

Which is why Ibadan is a city which writes its own history. In that history, every house is a griot, the streets are delicate footprints of telling seasons. J. P. Clark's inimitable eye sees Ibadan as a "running splash of rust and gold". As I pan this large city from the shadows of Mapo Hall, I ponder the touching accuracy of Clark's canvas, just as I envision a time when that running gold will have no place for any rust.

*   First written July 12, 1990; updated March 25, 1997.

Notes

1. There is a New Mbari (inaugurated in 1995) housed in the New Culture Studios complex, courtesy Demas Nwoko, owner of the complex and a prominent member of the Old Mbari. There is also a new British Council Library on Jericho Road, established by the Council and the Leventis Foundation.
2. Western Nigeria Broadcasting Service/Television.
3. Television Service of Oyo State.
4. Broadcasting Corporation of Oyo State.
5. Nigeria Broadcasting Corporation.
6. Federal Radio Corporation of Nigeria.
7. Galaxy Television, the first privately owned TV station in Ibadan, joined the ranks about two years ago.

YORUBA THOUGHT, ENGLISH WORDS:
A POET'S JOURNEY THROUGH THE TUNNEL OF TWO TONGUES

*Nobody who attempts to translate Yoruba into English
will doubt that 'poetry is what is left out in translation'
Ulli Beier[1]*

When two languages meet, they kiss and quarrel. They achieve a
tacit understanding on the common grounds of similarity and
convergence, then negotiate, often through strident rivalry and
self-preserving altercations, their areas of dissimilarity and
divergence. Phonology, the organizing component of the sound
and sounding system of a language, is a notorious bone of
contention in the quarrel between tongues. It is common
knowledge that by the time we are in our early teenage years, all
the speech organs are virtually set and adjusted to the realization
of the sounds they have been exposed to since early childhood.
Mastering the phonemes of other languages after this is still
possible, but at great pedagogical cost and enormous investment
of talent. This is why many Yoruba speakers often pronounce
"those' as "dose", "chew" as "shoe". English dental fricatives
and affricates simply do not exist in Yoruba. This is also why in
the mouth of an untrained English speaker, Yoruba words like

"rogbodiyan", "fiangbonfiangbon" "ajimatanrareje" are likely
to quarrel incoherently - and at times loudly enough to attract the
attention of the language police! The syllable isochronicity and
complex tone system of Yoruba are as much a tongue ache to the
English speaker as the stress and intonation patterns of English
are a constant worry to the Yoruba speaker.

But the burden of this presentation is "thought" which in the
language neighborhood, shares closer borders with semantics
than other components (although as we shall see shortly, in
Yoruba language and communicative pragmatics, sounding is
meaning and meaning is sounding). In the realm of incantatory
poetry, it is words—or rather their sounding—which provoke the
universal sympathies, make things happen or unhappen, intrude
the chanter's will upon the universe of the seen and unseen, and
convert that will into a demand and that demand into a command
which insists on fulfilment. For in the Yoruba imagination—and
pragmatics— words are abstract, innate and mute until given the
breath of the human voice, called forth, as it were, from it to *it-
ness*, from relative nothingness into being. The calling forth is
easier, more efficacious when the referent has a name, the name
being the product of a cooperative principle between verbal
signification and ontological identity. The name opens the door
to the house of being; it is the readiest, most direct channel to a
person's *ori* and all it stands for in the liturgy of existence. The
Yoruba believe that to endow something with a name is to give it
life beyond subsistence. This world did not exist until a word
existed in which its name was found. The world itself was
evoked into being by the proclamation of that name. To live is to
have a name; to have a name is to live.

What is "Yoruba Thought"? I can hear people asking. What
makes it different from Akan thought, Gikuyu thought, Xhoza
thought, English thought, German thought, etc.? Let me quickly
add a caveat here. This essay is not a philosophical foray into
Yoruba thought and thought systems, but rather an exploration of
the experiences of *one* Yoruba poet as regards the problems and
challenges involved in the expression of Yoruba ideas in
English. No ethnocentric or essentialist project is intended here,
no undue emphasis on the "uniqueness" of Yoruba language and
thought. However, there are enough ideational and verbal

dissimilarities between Yoruba and English to warrant their examination and exposition by a creative writer with a more than passing familiarity with both languages. For I believe that more than any other professional, the creative writer stands in an ideal position to serve as umpire in that quarrel that we talked about earlier on, though quite often he/she gets bruised in the scuffle and may suffer a broken rib or a swollen lip!

In umpiring this scuffle and describing its process I am doing nothing earthshakingly new. Gabriel Okara, poet and author of the inimitable novel called *The Voice*, once gave his own testimony on the Ijaw-English encounter; Chinua Achebe recorded the progress of the novelist's ideas from Igbo to English; while more recently Femi Oyebode took stock of the prosodic peculiarities of Yoruba poetry, hinting at the enormous problems involved in getting the English language to accommodate them.

A query of sorts may be raised at a personal level. How "Yoruba" now can the "thought" of this writer be—this writer who, though "Farmer-born, peasant-bred," has also, alas, got "classroom-bled"? This writer who, born and raised in the rich, awesomely green rainforest region of Nigeria, of Africa, has also lived and studied in Europe and America and interacted with the best—and at times the worst—paradigms of Western thought. This writer who has been deeply touched by the literatures and philosophies of the East (far, middle and near), Asia, and Latin America. This writer for whom the oceans are mere bowls of water into which *human* thoughts keep falling like rain drops. This writer whose rocks and rivers, hills and mountains are taller and larger than any frontier, whose pathways transcend the rigid contour of any map, whose geography is constantly mediated—interrogated—by history. I mean this writer has read—and studied—Shakespeare, Dostoevsky, Marx—even Hegel who denied Africa any claim to *weltgeist* and knocked a whole continent and its people out of the bewildering flux of human history.

Amazingly, the more universal this writer's umbrella has tended to be, the more intense has been the particularity of every speck of shade under it. The rainbow is so generally beautiful because of the astonishing brilliance of every color in its spectrum. In the end every color negotiates its own peculiarity with the eye, its own tenacity on the mind—but in a way that does not put the general spectrum into any disharmony. Where else can I seek my most immediate authority in this matter if not from a Yoruba proverb/poem:

Irú wá	*Iru* comes
Ògì ǹ wá	*Ogiri* reports
Ni ímó bèé dùn	That is how the stew becomes tasty
Sùgbon tani o mo	But who does not know
P'óto ladun iru	That *iru* has its taste
Oto ladun ogiri?	And *ogiri* has its own?

Yes, indeed, there are Yoruba ways of thinking which have produced a certain science of being, a certain blend of wisdom and philosophy, certain moral ideals and a certain epistemology—certain Yoruba ways of segmenting experience and cognising the world. No one ever possesses a whole town; you can only own a house (or more) in it. Even then between that town and the house is a relationship of mutual definition. Yoruba thoughts exist in relation to the world, achieving in many areas an unignorable degree of uniqueness. Yoruba language is the ideal, most natural medium for the articulation of those thoughts. What happens, then, when what is "thought" in Yoruba finds expression in English? What problems arise? What are the strategies for their mediation? What are the frustrations? What are the profits?

The two languages locked in this creative scuffle are Yoruba and English. Like all encounters between Africa and Europe, it is a "contest" between two unequal parties, a relationship between two unequal histories (no, historiographies!) and epistemologies. Although it cannot be said for sure which of the two languages "was born" first, that is, which of them predated the other in its oral essence, it is an incontestable fact that English does not only have a scribal precedence over Yoruba, Yoruba was, indeed reduced to writing by those already literate and versed in English letters and culture.[2] Needless to say, these pioneers of Yoruba orthography did not only approach the new language with the skill and insight gained from English, they also went to work on the "new" language with some of the prejudices, assumptions, and ethnocentric arrogance prevalent in their time. For not long ago, it was fashionable to distinguish between the "civilized" languages of Europe an the "primitive" tongues of the less industrialized parts of the world, the former having been assumed to possess a kind of expressive adequacy absent in the latter. Increasing fieldwork especially in descriptive and socio-linguistics and the opening of the world through more frequent travel and contact among its diverse peoples, have given the lie to these assumptions, but some languages still confront the world with the privilege and from the vantage point enjoyed over the centuries by their speakers. This is why for a long time Yoruba orthography had a noticeably Anglicised base, a situation which brings to mind the heroic struggle of English itself to break out of the mold of Latin grammar.

Yoruba's early contact was not only with speakers of European languages; it was, most significantly, with English speakers who were also Christian missionaries. Their translation into Yoruba of the Bible, the major hymns and other Christian texts left a remarkable imprint on the target language—and its culture. It also manifested both the bias and ignorance of the translators. Perhaps in no other instance is the cultural and epistemic politics of missionary translation more blatant than in the rendering of the Yoruba word "*babalawo*" (*dibia* in Igbo). English "equivalents" such as "sorcerer", "fetish priest", "witch doctor", "juju priest" were enthusiastically employed by translators who saw their act as an opportunity to undermine the very significant place of the *babalawo* in Yoruba belief.[3] It must be borne in mind that Christianity is a monotheistic, this-*not*-that faith, whereas Yoruba traditional religion at whose center the *babalawo* stands, is plural, this-*and*-that. In other words, while the former operates by replacive progression, the latter is essentially additive in true conformity with the Yoruba saying, *Oju orun tegberun eyee fo laifarakanra* (the sky is wide enough for a thousand birds to fly without having to compete for space).

It has to be admitted that even under normal, neutral, circumstances, words like '*babalawo*' do not surrender to easy rendering across languages. A highly multi-faceted, multifunctional figure, the *babalawo* is a doctor, physician, psycho-therapist, occultist, priest, diviner, griot, historian, bard, community leader, etc. How can one grab a word or phrase that can capture these diverse facets at one and the same time especially in another language, in another culture? As far as I know, the closest to a satisfactory equivalent has been 'diviner-physician' by Kofi Awoonor[4]; but then, that covers only two aspects of the babalawo's complex profile.

Evangelical translation fosters further tendentious approximations and misrepresentations. For example, the Christian Satan is often taken as the equivalent of the Yoruba Esu, whereas while the former is monochromatically evil and condemned to eternal perdition, the latter is the agent of ambivalence and mischief, the one who complicates the plot in the narrative of Fate, a god with a prominent place in the Yoruba pantheon. Also, in an arrogantly Manichean vein, sharers of the Christian faith see themselves as "*Onigbagbo*" ('Believers') while those outside their fold are regarded as "unbelievers". I have never stopped wondering what dictionary supplies the Christian definition of "belief" and "unbelief", and the vectors of these two states of being. I have never stopped wondering why, how, faith in the Christian god and his angels amounts to "belief", while faith in Osun, Ogun, Sango etc. is so haughtily dismissed as "unbelief". But I have always marveled at the hypocrisy at work when statuettes and figurines of "holy" personages are preserved and revered in the Catholic Church while carvings and sculptures embodying the essence of Yoruba deities are renounced as "idols" and dumped in the pyre by proselytising clerics, or carted away as prized artifacts by foreign adventurers.

Enough of tendentious translations and their sanctimonious masks. Over now to a different plane where that quarrel between languages and cultures is more secular even if not less aggressive. As we hinted earlier on, all human languages in the world share common boundaries in some areas; and suffer behind sundering walls in others. Despite the linguistic universals and trans-lingual commonalities that have come into prominence in recent times, it is still common knowledge that each language possesses its own uniqueness, each language maintains—and frequently defends— its own territory of sounding and meaning. Of the three components of language, phonology provides the area in which that uniqueness is most clearly— and most frustratingly—prominent. In the specific instance of Yoruba and English, this is where the translator's task is most daunting, most forbidding. For while English is a stress-timed language, Yoruba is a syllable-timed one operating through a complex system of tones and glides. In this language prosody mellows into melody. Sounding is meaning, meaning is sounding. The music which emanates from the soul of words is an inalienable part of the beauty of the tongue. Tone is the power-point, the enabling element in a Yoruba communicative event. And Yoruba's tonal pattern is so intrinsic, so indigenous to the language, thus confronting any trans-lingual mediator with a frustrating problem. Let us illustrate with these two sayings:

(a)   Iṣẹ́ loogun iṣẹ́
        (*Hard work* is the cure for *poverty*)

(b)   Ọrọ rere a maa yọ obi ninu apo
        Ọrọ búburú ni i yọ ọfà ninu apó
        (Good words draw out kolanuts from the *pocket*
        Bad words invite arrows from the *quiver*).

The meaning and epigrammatic force of these statements derive from the delicate tonal contrast in the Yoruba original:

iṣẹ́	versus	iṣẹ́
(hard work)		(poverty)

Ọrọ rere :	apo	:versus	ọrọ búburú	apó
good words:	pocket	:	bad words	quiver

Note that in the Yoruba original, the contrast is at two levels: phonological and lexico-semantic, whereas that contrast can be realized only at the lexico-semantic level in the English rendering. Needless to say, most of the drama of expression and meaning, of sounding and signifying secreted in the original is lacking in the English version. This kind of disparity is even more pronounced in a text like the following:

Ojú mọ́, n ò gbọ́ *poroporo* odó
Oganjọ́ gan, n ò gbó *wọsọwọsọ* konkọsọ
N o gbọ *sinrinkunsinkun* ká din eku méye
A faimò k'áwo má sun l'ébi, afaimọ

What a morning, when the air is not filled with the
clang of pounding yam!
What an evening, when I listened in vain to them
sift the flour!
When the frying-pots do not simmer with the
fricassee of rabbits and birds,
What an outlook, when the expert retires under the
shadow of starvation![5]

Here we confront onomatopoiea, an eminently common Yoruba
feature, at its most triumphant intricacy. '*Poroporo*' the sound of
the pestle in the mortar, '*wọsọwọsọ*', the sound of the sifting of
flour, '*sinrinkunsinkun*', the sizzling of frying meat are all sound
images which transmit their meanings by evoking the drama of
the referential process. These are words which name *(onoma)*
poetically *(poeia)* by conjuring up the physicality of the referring
scene. They take us by the hand (or ear as the case may be) and
lead us through sensuous and sensory corridors to the arena of
re-lived experience, from aural reality to visual imagination.
They are abstract symbols with concrete underpinnings. Also
significant here is the indirectness, the suggestiveness of the
communicative process: although no food item is directly
mentioned, we are able to deduce through the collocation of
poroporo + *odo*, and *wọsọwọsọ* + *konkọsọ* that pounded yam
(which is invariably the 'dough of contention' between pestle
and mortar!) and *àmàlà* (food made from yam or plantain flour)
are the ultimate objects of reference.

At the prosodic level, there is a text-wide tone distribution in
the poem. As E. L. Lasebikan has observed, the mixed tones
encountered in the first three lines are underscored and made
more sober by the grave effect produced by the repetition of the
word '*àf'àimò*' (all low, grave tones) on the last line. Even in
these four lines of verse, there is a complex interplay of words, a

pattern of chant and music so indigenous to Yoruba that they can hardly enjoy faithful transposition into any other language. This verbal interplay and its attendant music are fostered by a phono-syntactic peculiarity resulting from the cognate formation of the verb '*gàn*' from the noun '*òganjó*'.[6] Phonological repetition is enhanced by syntactic economy, a process so intricately Yoruba that it becomes the translator's nightmare.

A similar phonological obstacle stands between the following song and a wholesome rendering in English:

> *Kogó kogó* la ngbo'un *agogo*
> *Gèdè gèdè* ni *t'akèrègbè*;
> B' àkèrègbè ti tóbi tó
> Ko l'óhùn agogo l'ẹnu.

> *Kogó kogó* is the sound of the iron gong
> *Gèdè gèdè* is that of the gourd
> Big as the gourd is
> It can never sound like the gong.

The above song operates through an intricate tonal and semantic counterpoint.[7] The MIDDLE-HIGH MIDDLE-HIGH tone in '*Kogó kogó*' is complemented by the MIDDLE MIDDLE MIDDLE tone in '*agogo*'; and both are counterpointed by the LOW-LOW-LOW-LOW tone in '*gèdè gèdè*' and the three LOW tones in '*akèrègbè*'. Here, again, we have another 'sound investment'. The positive quality of '*agogo*' resides in its high-pitched sound, which contrasts markedly with the wingless softness suggested by '*akèrègbè's' 'gèdè gèdè*'. All these sound contrasts are built around an ironic reversal of sizes: the big, round *akèrègbè* is so haplessly outvoiced by the small, narrow *agogo* in a competition for the ear! Unfortunately all this drama and the sound contrast which provides its plot and *dramatis personae* can hardly cross the translation bridge without sacrificing something at the first end.

Yoruba owes a large portion of its lexicon to ideophones, those sound images and sound symbols which mediate the rhythm of speech into the movement of meaning. Words proceed from the cradle of the tongue, dance suggestively through the streets of the ears, baiting or biting as they dance along. Without doubt, Yoruba's phonological space remains the poet's most fertile, most challenging, and most indulgent terrain. It also remains the translator's intractable ordeal. For, as Phillips[8] has most appropriately remarked, Yoruba remains the missing link between music and speech.

Other mediation problems of the lexico-semantic type abound. As we said earlier on, different languages do not only segment experience in different ways, they have different ways of expressing the same experience. Consider these two ways of pointing attention to an empty stomach:

(a)   Ebi npa mí (Yoruba)
(b)   I am hungry (English)

It is a matter for eternal debate if (b) is a wholesome translation of (a). In other words, are these two utterances saying the "same" thing? Are they denotatively and affectively identical? A word-for-word, literal translation of (a) will guide us towards an answer:

	Ebi	nṕa	mí
(c)	Hunger	is killing beating	me

Needless to say, (b) can only be a sense or idiomatic translation of (a). For while (b) is abstract and colorless, (c) concretises the experience and its expression complete with its physicality and drama. Syntactically, in (b) the object or affected is spatially foregrounded through its initial position in the sentence, while the psychological subject of affector is silenced, omitted, or taken for granted; in (a) the allocation of roles is more clear. 'Ebi' is subject or affector while 'mi' is object or affected. 'Ebi' registers its (anti-) heroic prominence in the utterance by its initial position, and as a noun, while in (b) 'hungry' has been class-shifted to the station of an ordinary predicative adjective. Utterances (a) and (b) are, therefore, equivalents only to a certain degree.

Many Yoruba words frustrate trans-lingual transposition by the sheer complexity of their polysemic range. An engaging example is the word *ori*:

(a)   *Orí ńfọ́ mi* (My *head* is aching)
(b)   *Ori mi pe* (My *head* is correct, i.e. I am intelligent)
(c)   *Orí yọ mi* (Head delivered me, i.e. My God saved me)
(d)   *Mo l' órí púpọ̀* (I have plenty of head, i.e. plenty of luck)
(e)   *Orí mi dára* (My *head* is good, i.e. I am fortunate).[9]

It must be admitted that even in English the word "head" is highly polysemic (*head* of department; head of cattle; matters come to a head, etc.), but none of these comes close to the metaphysical possibilities of '*ori*' in Yoruba language and culture. Like the Igbo *chi, ori* may refer to personal god, guardian spirit, life force, protective essence, etc. According to Yoruba belief, at creation, and at *akunleyan* (the divine moment of choice) each individual selects the *ori* which shapes his/her destiny on life's long and mysterious journey. For the one who picks *ori ire* (good head), life will turn out to be a happy, prosperous fare, while the hapless chooser of *ori buruku* (bad head) will find life an interminable bout of sadness and failure. *Ori* then remains one's own little universe which is itself the door to the larger universe of being. It is that little but vital god who must hearken to and answer one's prayer before Olodumare can give assent. It is the spirit which leads for us to follow, just as most of us did at birth, on our way from the womb. The Yoruba, therefore, have a way of differentiating the head we see (the head without) from the head we cannot see (the god within), hence the common prayer:

> *Ki orí inú wa maa ba t'òde jẹ́*
> (May our inside head never spoil the outside one).

Ontological concepts like *ori* are so culture-bound that they do not translate easily across languages, especially when their metaphysical polyvalence in the source language has no equivalent in the target language. When this happens, translation yields place to mediation as the literary communicator is constrained to try out or devise a series of strategies of transposition and transference. Copious explanatory notes and elaborations are employed to cushion the strange item in its target location, though accusations of quaintness still linger, as happened when an English reader of my acquaintance encountered these two lines which serve as refrain in my poem *"Awure"*:

>Wherever my head leads my feet today
>Let all paths open like a book of seeing sands

*　　*　　*　　*　　*　　*　　*

How does one conceive, think out, a poem in Yoruba, then give it expression in English? If language is truly the dress of thought, how would deeply Yoruba ideas look and feel in English coat and tie? What adjustments must be made in size and style to prevent the tie from turning into a noose? It must be admitted straightaway that English is a highly flexible and accommodating language. Everywhere in the world, its syntax is being bent (not broken), its lexicon expanded with new, exciting entries, its semiotic range widened and deepened beyond the ken—and control—of its native speakers. The language is boosted - and bruised - in the process: this is the prize it does get, and the price it must pay as an international language whose imposition and spread was effected by the gunboat in many parts of the world. But no matter how flexible, English is English. Yoruba is Yoruba. What does the writer then do to make sure that the twain shall meet? What bridges does he/she devise; what strategies of appeasement? This last segment of the essay will involve my personal testimonies.

Yoruba is my mother tongue, English my acquired language. The former brings warm intimations of the cradle and the homestead, the latter stern memories of the classroom and the blackboard. In Yoruba, poetry is song and chant, a performed or performable *event* throbbing with human breath, with a robust sense of audience and participation. Accomplishment in the art is still largely natural, a matter of talent, or lineage inheritance; it is still demotic, if not democratic. Illiterate village women chant *oriki* (praise poetry, panegyric)[10] with a virtuosity that would make a university professor of poetry go blank with envy; traditional hunters regale one another with *ijala* (hunters' song) from sundown till the last cock at dawn has crowed. At the personal level, I grew up admiring my father's performance of *alamo* (a long, colourful, episodic song popular among the Ekiti-Yoruba).

So poetry for me is song, performance; it is utter-ance. In the beginning was not the Word, in the Word was the Beginning. But the Word was a tablet of letters and symbols, mute and immobile until endowed with the animating power of the human voice. Meaning is sounding, sounding meaning. But how have I been meaning in Yoruba and sounding in English?

Through phonological and prosodic approximations[11] exemplified in the generous use of alliteration, assonance, and consonance in the English text. Through the use of repetition and various reiterative strategies which may sometimes look (but hardly *sound*) pleonastic in the eye of some readers. Critics who condemn these devices in my poetry, I suspect, are those trained to read poetry, not hear it; those who are used to locating the prosodic climax of the poem only in the rhymes at the tail end of its lines. Rhythm for me is systemic and pervasive. It is secreted in every consonant and every vowel even as both engage in the musical union that begets the syllable. The Yoruba syllable is a unit of music. To reflect its glides and slurs in English I often go for long-drawing words, hence the ubiquity of words with the -ing ending in my verse. I am more of an ear than an eye poet. On certain desperate occasions when a quarrel erupts between the sounding and the meaning of a word, I often tilt the scale in favour of the former.

I strongly believe that common sounds can be invested with new meanings (and vice versa?) even beyond the institutionalized matrix of onomatopoeia. An exploration of that belief led to the following stanza:

> some into *gba*
> some into *gbu*
> some into the *gbaagbuu*
> of Mehunmutapa[12]

The interpretation of *gba* and *gbu* must start in the mouth before preceding to the brain! The heaviness of the labio-velar plosive /gb/; the contrasting realization of the open vowel /a/ and the close /u/; the coming together of both syllables and lengthening (through doubling) of both vowels in *gbaagbuu* is all intended to produce an oral-aural bang with a resonance which reaches back to primordial times with their pagan winds and feathered legends. Signified here is the inevitability of diversity (*gba* versus *gbu*) and the necessity of unity (*gbaagbuu*) within a liberating context of the sense of common origins (Mehunmutapa). I have always been fascinated and intrigued by what sounds were like before human beings invested them with their polyglot meanings.

Sounds matter. So do the syntactic patternings which endow them with anchor and sequence. One sub-genre of Yoruba poetry which exploits most mellifluously the intricate interplay of sound patterning and syntactic patterning is *oriki*, the most basic, most widely practised of all Yoruba poetic types of the secular variety. It is a genre I have cherished since my childhood (my paternal grandmother was an impressive *oriki* chantress), a genre which has wielded an unmistakable influence on my poetic style. But *oriki* is a breeding ground and storehouse of the tropes of attribute. Its seriated noun clauses, relative clauses, and interminable appositional phrases thrive in the liberal syntactic structure of Yoruba. To transpose them into English, I have found it necessary to syncopate here, reduce the number of appositional clauses there, then adjust for sounding and rhetorical appropriateness. The result looks like the following excerpts:

> Iroko wears the crown of the forest,
> town's rafter, roof of the forest
> ironwood against the termites of time
> Iroko wears the crown of the forest
> its baobab foot rooted against
> a thousand storms.

> Iroko wears the crown of the forest,
> Scourge of the sweating sawyer

the champion matchet assays a bite,
beating a blunted retreat to the whetting stone.
The ironwood wears the crown of the forest.[13]

If the hearer/reader finds the iron piece on *iroko* too hard to
swallow, s/he may seek solace in the tastiness of the following:

Give me wine, palm wine,
Sap of the honey tree
Give me wine, palm wine,
Raffia miracle of watersides
Give me wine, palm wine
The unmatchable maiden
Who turns valiant suitors
Into tapping lizards
Give me wine, palm wine,
The hasty god in the patient keg,[14]

At times, the subject is autobiographical; the tone takes the form
of declarative introduction:

I am child of the river, child of the rock
Child, of rock hills holding hands
Above the tallest roofs.
Dawns are grey, dusks brown:
Whoever craves the blue legend of Ikere skies,
Let him turn his neck like a barber's chair[15]

In these and similar cases, I am painfully aware of the
difference between the Yoruba chant in my mind, and the
English poem that is born after laborious midwifing; of the long
journey between a song summoned from memory by the urgency
of the human voice and a poem committed to cold print with its
scribal rigidity. I am aware of the liberty I am taking with
English syntax, of the expansion and liberalization that must take
place before a structural space now almost completely given to
the lean and competent verse can concede some room to the
vibrant lyricism of the song of the marketplace and the village
square. Most times the innate flexibility of the English language

rallies to my assistance, but I have tried not to push it beyond its elastic limit.

Just like translation, mediation has its limit. Very frequently I am confronted by the problem of transposing Yoruba metaphors, idioms, concepts and allusions which have no equivalence in English. In this regard, the highly agglutinative and meaning-laden Yoruba names are particularly intractable. And yet, like 'Mosáfẹ́jọ́' in *Waiting Laughters*[16]; 'Ẹsimúdà' in *Village Voices*[17]; "Madàrú' and 'Ayederu' in *Songs of the Marketplace*[18], these names are necessary for a full interpretation and comprehension of the poems in which they occur. One of my coping strategies is to transfer such problematic items into English, most times with footnotes and glossary. These strategies can hardly settle the quarrel between the two languages, but they frequently achieve a truce.

*   *   *   *   *   *   *

Yoruba and English. I do not only write in these two languages. I also live in them. I am close enough to hear their amorous chuckles and bitter bickerings. Poetry comes more naturally to me in Yoruba: the words dance to the drum of the heart; the lines pluck their beat from the rhythm of the mind. Mediating all this in English is a problem which has long become a challenge. Most times I inhabit the interface between these two tongues, arriving with idioms which to some ears may sound quaint or unusually fresh. I explore that interface, keenly aware of the pragmatic necessity of English without losing sight of the vital primacy of Yoruba. It is an acutely problematic interface, one that constantly reminds me that there is no wholly satisfactory alternative to creating and performing Yoruba poetry in its indigenous medium.

Notes

1. Ulli Beier, "On Translating Yoruba Poetry" (introduction to) *Yoruba Poetry: An Anthology of Traditional Poems.* Cambridge University Press, 1970, pp. 11-25.

2. J. F. Ade Ajayi, "How Yoruba Was Reduced to Writing". *Odu: Journal of Yoruba, Edo, and Related Studies*, No. 8, 1960, pp. 49-58.
3. Niyi Osundare, "Bilingual and Bicultural Aspects of Nigerian Prose Fiction". Ph.D. Dissertation, York University, Toronto, Canada, 1979; see also "Caliban's Gamble: Stylistic Repercussions of Writing African Literature in English". K. Owolabi (ed.), *Language in Nigeria: Essays in Honour of Ayo Bamgbose*. Ibadan: Group Publishers, 1995, pp. 340-363.
4. Kofi Awoonor, *The Breast of the Earth*. New York: Anchor Press, 1975.
5. E. L. Lasebikan, "Tone in Yoruba Poetry", *Odu: Journal of Yoruba and Related Studies*, Vol. 7, No. 2, 1964, pp. 35-38.
6. I owe this observation to the insight of Dr. Kola Owolabi of the Department of Linguistics and African Languages, University of Ibadan, Nigeria.
7. See O. Olatunji, "Characteristic Features of Yoruba Oral Poetry". Ph.D. Thesis, University of Ibadan, Nigeria, 1971.
8. In Ulli Beier *op. cit.* p. 11.
9. Niyi Osundare, "Bilingual and Bicultural Aspects of Nigerian Prose Fiction", p.145.
10. Karin Barber, *I Could Speak Until Tomorrow: Oriki, Women, and the Past in a Yoruba Town*. Edinburgh University Press, 1991.
11. See Femi Oyebode, "Prosody and Literary Texts", *The Pressures of the Text*. Stewart Brown ed., Birmingham University (U.K.) African Studies Series, No. 4, pp. 91-95.
12. Niyi Osundare, *Midlife*. Ibadan: Heinemann Educational Books, 1993, p. 10.
13. Niyi Osundare, *The Eye of the Earth*. Ibadan: Heinemann Educational Books, 1986, p. 5.
14. Niyi Osundare, *Song of the Season*. Ibadan: Heinemann Educational Books, 1990, p. 55.
15. Niyi Osundare, *Midlife*. Ibadan: Heinemann Educational Books, 1993, p. 11.
16. Niyi Osundare, *Waiting Laughters*. Lagos & Oxford: Malthouse, 1990, p. 75.
17. Niyi Osundare, *Village Voices*. Ibadan: Evans Brothers, 1984, pp. 46 & 57.
18. Niyi Osundare, *Songs of the Marketplace*. Ibadan: New Horn, 1983, pp. 34 & 37.

*THRESHOLDS AND MILLENNIAL CROSSINGS

If someone had predicted about four decades ago that on this threshold of the 21st century, I would be the privileged recipient of a great honor from one of France's most prestigious universities, I would have advised that prophet to hang his cassock and drop his bell in the sea. For at that time, at that impressionable stage of my educational career, my eloquent desire to add French to my linguistic repertoire suffered a deafening defeat as my school was too young, too ill-equipped, to start a French programme. So I concentrated my attention on Yoruba, my mother tongue, and Latin, then the reigning academic language in Nigerian "Grammar Schools".

But that was not the end of my desire to learn French. At the higher school certificate level, and now at a much older, much richer school, I enrolled in an evening French class where we parroted "Je m'appelle... Je m'appelle..." after an overworked but enthusiastic teacher who rewarded us with tons and tons of "C'est bon... C'est bon", while the entire class chanted "O ma cherie o ma cherie/ Ecoute moi, ecoute moi" with a gusto that nearly brought down the roof. Our teacher did not miss one moment in telling us that French was the language of civilization

(I remembered my English teacher had also said the same thing about her own language!), that the French laid much store by the health of their language, particularly its lexical and phonological integrity, that French was not just a language but an entire way of life. But soon the music stopped: our teacher returned to her country; we all got overwhelmed by our main academic programmes, and "O ma cherie" became a distant echo. My early attempt to cross the threshold between Yoruba and French thus received a setback. C'est fini?

Not quite. The window momentarily closed on my access to French language was thrown wide open in my history and literature classes. Here, the phenomena that have made a lasting impact on me and many of my colleagues are not just France's wars of conquest and expansion, her triumphs and defeats, her legendary diplomacy; not the precocious feminism of Joan of Arc, the "Golden Age" glories of Duc de Richelieu, the imperial prowess of Napoleon Bonaparte, or the martial democracy of Charles de Gaulle. What kept our minds engaged and constantly wondering was the French Revolution, its remote and immediate causes, particularly the remote. We entered The Social Contract with Jean Jacques Rousseau, explored *The Enlightenment* and probed *The Spirit of the Laws* with Montesquieu, spelt out and glossed the spirit of the age with Diderot and the Encyclopaedists. Convinced that these were the winds that powered the wheels of the French Revolution, we became abundantly aware of the power of mind over matter, the necessity, even indispensability, of ideas in the process of change, and the slow, painful, often imperceivable incubation of epochal events.

The vicissitudes of the Revolution itself: its triumphs and travails, its numerous trials and errors, its countless loyalties and betrayals, its unexpected, if not totally ironic twists and turns, its alarming capacity for eating up its own children, its eventual triumphs, its demonstration of the irrepressibility of the human spirit, its universal anthem of liberte, egalite, fraternite—all these registered themselves as France's immortal contributions to History, to the legacy of human struggle and freedom. And in our own neo-colonial condition and atmosphere of repressive military dictatorship, these three ideals of the French Revolution crystallised into a veritable philosophy about liberty and the humanization of the social and political space. Not only in our own country, not only on our own continent, but in the entire world as we saw it at that time. Although many of us kept wondering how a country which snatched these remarkable ideals out of the heat of revolutionary fire could later go on to colonize other countries and lay claim to the destiny of other peoples, we were keenly aware that the French had impacted History in a prodigiously fundamental way by producing a revolution that would become a mega text for other revolutions. In many ways, the French Revolution served as the harbinger for the republicanization of Western polities. It is a threshold of epocal proportions.

The throbbing echoes of the French Revolution have always been close to the inner ears of my radical consciousness. Thus, in one of the poems in my volume *Waiting Laughters* (a poem which I actually wrote on July 14, 1989 as my own little commemoration of the bicentinneal of the French Revolution), my mind crossed the threshold of two histories, two geographies, and two cultures:

> Waiting
> like the Bastille, for the screaming stones of turbulent streets;
> their bread is stone
> their dessert garnished sand from the kitchen of hearthless seasons
> And when the humble axe finally heeds its noble task, the head
> Descends, lumpen dust in its royal mouth
>
> Behold the wonder:
> the crown is only a cap![1]

The royal victim of this axe found a historical parallel in the annals of Ikere-Ekiti, my hometown, which once forced the banishment of a haughty, tyrannical oba. But there was a difference in the instruments which effected the change: while the French guillotine was a steel weapon with a ferocious edge, the Ikere guillotine was made up of satirical songs and ballads, a dreadful genre of orin ote (chants of subversion) which turned the palace into a poisoned lake, and the offending oba a hapless fish forced to thrash his way out. Thus a royal line was severed, but not a royal neck. According to a Yoruba saying, there are different ways of killing a fowl.

There are other trans-textualities, less ground-shaking, less sanguinary, but no less enduring. The French language did not come to me through the door; but its literature did come through the window of translated texts (bless translators, those healers of rift, those stitches in the rent tongues of Babel, bridge-builders, threshold crossers). Through their magic of mediation, I can wail with Phedre, laugh at Tartuffe, wander in the surreal wilderness of Rimbaud and Valery, gather petals of passion from the fabulous gardens of Baudelaire, survive the barricade with the Orphean flute of Jean-Paul Sartre, still threshing the wheat of Being from the shaft of Nothingness. I encounter Descartes wrapped up in an African proverb, his wit suffused with wonder, his syllogism endowed with a fourth premise, his cogito a cognomen of infinite laakaye2, his tome an open palm of ancestral hands illuminated by coordinate crossings and epic planes. The kindred sage I met on the way to my village stream flashed me a smile crisp like a water lily, then proclaimed with infectious aplomb: I am, therefore, I think.

Being before cognition, life before logic, soul and sense, tribe and text; then the supreme ontological bonding without which all philosophising is but reified idleness: I am, therefore, you are. You are, therefore, I am. How else do we talk about thresholds if not through a communality of living, through channels of existence, through the universe of being, infinite interpenetrations, mutual dependencies, contiguities of memory, geographies of awareness? What are thresholds if not contradictions which harden or dissolve into perplexing verities: near yet so far, fixed and free, narrow as a slit in Time's garment, yet wide as the sky, entrance and exit, gulf and bridge, light and darkness, memory and oblivion, end and beginning.... Thresholds are fluid in their complex territoriality: close enough to be private, even intimate, yet sufficiently exterior to lay claim to the patrimony of the public sphere.

Any wonder then that in some parts of Yorubaland, atewole (the-place-you-tread-before-you-enter-the-house) or enu ona (literally: the lip of the road) is regarded as sacred and regularly propitiated? The threshold is the interface territory between the myriad, trackless forces of the outside sphere and the sheltered, restricted ones of the interior. The interaction between these two spheres, these two sets of forces is watched with cosmic vigilance; for when they clash and quarrel within the household, the inhabitants know they owe an urgent sacrifice to Esu, the Yoruba god of mischief and happenstance, denizen of the crossroads, who frequently wreaks havoc at enu ona. Hence a bride coming home to the husband for the first time is made to halt at the threshold where her feet, shoeless, are washed, no, cleansed with water taken from a pitcher in the inner room; this is where prayers are said, and marriage counsel provided by older women who crossed that threshold long before. Passage through that ritual space becomes a transition from one house/family to another, from girlhood to womanhood and wifehood, an advancement into a new status and its accompanying battery of roles. In this vital crossing, the passage is alive with its own song, dance, and ritual password. More thresholds: the Yoruba recognize and revere the lips as the threshold of the temple of the mouth, that repository and vent for the Word; iponri (forehead) is honoured as passageway to ori (the main head); the toes as swift heralds of the foot. On a merrier, more secular level, an enchanting aroma is regarded as threshold to a hearty dish, a robust smile as overture to a willing heart, the thighs as prologue to the delicious drama in the arena below the navel....

There are so many other thresholds without portals: between life and death, death and life; the tadpole outgrows its tail and fattens into a frog; the colt steadies its gait and gallops into a thoroughbred; the ripening moon pursues the night to the threshold of dawn.... And our age, this last whimper of the 20th century, this age of hype and hurry, so drunk on contemporaneist bravado, that it sees nothing except in terms "posts": post-modernist, post-structuralist, post-Marxist, post-feminist, post-industrial, post-colonial, etc. Many of us seem to have crossed the bridge even without getting there. I have asked myself times without number: what kind of theoretical and critical thresholds can we cross with a baggage of concepts and postulations which only define themselves in terms of their having come after their pre-decessors? How much originality, indeed, can such a position lay claim to or concede? How clean, how clear are the vaunted breaks with the past; what is the semantic nationality of the prefix "post"; what, whose temporal passport does it carry; how does it define itself?

As we have seen earlier on, the threshold is the locus of indeterminacy and decision, point and perimeter, sound and silence. It is both space, clamorous in its physicality and yet so affecting in its telluric silence. It is a grey zone whose tone is deeper than other colors. Like the bridge that it is, it looks forward by looking back; it looks back by looking forward. And what time, what moment, for centennial/millennial stocktakng can be more appropriate than now as we perch nervously on the end of one century/millennium and the beginning of another? What more opportune juncture to examine humanity's journey so far, and hazard a mind-map for the epoch about to unfold?

The millennium in whose twilight we stand has been nothing short of thronged and turbulent. Feuding fiefdoms have warred or wangled their way into less contentious political arrangements. Tribes and disparate nationalities once described as mere geographical expressions have scrambled into nation states. In many places, absolute monarchs who owned their states and all therein and whose word once carried the power of life and death, have softened into constitutional figureheads, the parliament having supplanted the palace. (How so often we forget that democracy as we know it today is a young and still growing phenomenon!) Wars of aggression and territorial expansion have largely abated thanks to the courage, sacrifice, and resilience of dominated peoples, the insistent goodness of progressive people all over the world, the advancement of diplomacy and the development of other ways of making war. Empires have risen, declined, and fallen. The primitive passion to conquer and dominate other human beings is being tamed as homo sapiens is struggling desperately to justify the sapiens in its nomenclature. As regards my own part of the world, Africa's travails began about the middle of the out-going millennium:

from the savage plunder of slavery and the slave trade, to the dispossession of colonialism, and now the remote-control strategems of neo-colonialism—all with their consequent racism and the pervasive dehumanization of peoples of African origin, all with debilitating repercussions rearing to cross the threshold to the next millennium. Will humanity grant them a ticket? Will Africa go through another century with her peoples still the wretched of the earth?

If the out-going millennium/century has not been very kind to humanity, it is surely because humanity has not been kind to it. It has been a war-torn, blood-stained period, blemished by intolerance and hate. Take the 20th century as a case in point. The First World War (for that is what historians like to call it) cost over 14 million human lives. Humanity was just reeling out of the spell of that catastrophe when World War II announced its coming, its casualties almost double those of its predecessor, complete with the traumatising evil of the Holocaust. The theatres of war and waste would later include Korea and Vietnam, the killing fields of Somalia, Rwanda, and Kosovo....

But there have been a few silver linings in the millennial cloud. The period also witnessed astonishing scientific breakthroughs and near-miraculous discoveries. The invention of penicillin strengthened the human being's ammunition against disease; the battle against the tyranny of distance was won with incredibly fast and efficient means of communication; the atom was split and in its mysterious core was found the key to thousands of scientific wonders. The computer made its triumphal advent, a long-sought helpmate to the human brain. This is also the millennium of Adam Smith and Karl Marx, Mao Zedong and Mandela, Ataturk and Gandhi, Joan of Arc and Nzinga, Walt Whitman and Pablo Neruda, William Shakespeare and Wole Soyinka; of Charles Gaulle, Abraham Lincoln, Eleanor Roosevelt, Sigmund Freud, W.E.B. Du Bois, Chinua Achebe, Leonardo da Vinci, Pablo Picasso, Beethoven, Albert Einstein, The Beatles and Fela Anikulaapo-Kuti. It is also an era when the Brave New World appeared to have truly arrived. The human being called the bluff of planetary mystery and the first earthly foot surprised the craggy surface of the Moon.

A long, thronged period of stars and scars. As we stay poised at this historic juncture, it seems proper to ask a few basic questions which ever so often we ignore or are too busy to notice in a world increasingly afflicted by multiple dissonance and metallic noises. Call them my "threshold questions" if you wish: How much of the out-going millennium/century should we take with us to the incoming one? How much of it should we jettison so as to be able to keep afloat on the next millennial raft? Will the primitive propensity to conquer, subjugate, exploit... trail us into the new millennium? Will the new epoch produce its own Hitler, its own Pinochet, its own Abacha? Shall we enter that period still trapped in the castles of our skins, shackled by the sundry cruelties of the expiring era? And science and technology, our useful though troublesome servants in this century, will they become our masters in the coming one? In particular, will the coming millennium really witness the cloning of the human being: will Dolly the Wooly Magic have a human cousin? Will the atom complete its mission and ride humanity's hubris to an apocalypse of dust and ashes? Just where will our progeny be, and how will they look, at the end of the coming era? To reiterate, how much of this millennium should we take to the new one; how much must we leave behind?

Questions. More questions. For what are thresholds if not loci of interrogation, if not tropes of doubts and darings? If humanity had asked the right questions at the outset of the out-going millennium, maybe our world would later have reaped a harvest of healthier answers. This juncture offers us the rare chance to anticipate and forestall, to empower prophecy with hindsight. For divination is always healthier than postmortem.... But in hazarding these questions, am I not sounding exasperatingly out of place in a "post-moralist", "post-humanist" age? Maybe my cultural and ideological background has something to do with clamorous insistence. I come from that part of the world where the poem is a song which draws its lifeblood from the mouth-to-mouth respiration of communal bonding, a place where listeners still ask at the end of the story "alright, well told, but what does your story teach us?". Hence poems still function as "verbal guillotines", and a well-aimed ballad may ignite the cabinet of a rotten government. Literature matters; literature matters utterly.

Itself a repository of crossroads and thresholds, it facilitates the transgression of boundaries and subversion of hegemonic rigidities. And what has African literature been doing in the past one thousand years if not crossing boundaries and assaulting walls imposed by History upon the horizon of the continent whose aspirations it has been striving to articulate? As a writer, I consider mine an answerable imagination which responds to the urgency and inevitability of that historic mission. Primary on my mind, central to my art, is that urge to put Humanity first, illuminate the threshold between past and present, language and silence, thought and action, self and Other, Africa and the world - an urge which has found expression in a poem I have performed so many times and in so many places now that it is beginning to sound like my own threshold song:

I WANT TO TOUCH THE WORLD

I am possessed by an urge to touch the world
An urge keener than dawn's breeze
insuppressible like a stubborn faith

To fling a bridge across the seas
Tell every mountain a humble tale
Watch trees join roots below the earth

To sing in the east and dance in the west
To have the moon join the sun
Skycentre, without an eclipse
To trade passionate breaths across the hill
Where voices remember their echoes
Sowing pigeons in the wind

To see the ocean in a drop of water
The rainbow union of sun and rain
The road which runs from door to door

I want to kiss a thousand stamps
Moisten countless envelopes in their flighty tongues
Lace every shore with urgent tidings

I am possessed by an urge to touch the clouds
Tickle every dream in its armpit
Golden link in a horizontal chain of being

I am a lowly vine reaching for the light
Hand of night, alive with fingers
An adjective waiting for a noun.[3]

* A slightly modified version of the Acceptance Speech at the conferment of the degree of Doctor of Philosophy *honoris causa* by l'Universite de Toulouse-le Mirail, February 4, 1999.

Notes

1. Niyi Osundare. *Waiting Laughters*. Lagos & Oxford: Malthouse Press, 1990, p. 22.
2. A Yoruba word meaning intelligence, wisdom, resourcefulness, all rolled into one; it is superior to mere knowledge or competence.
3. Niyi Osundare. *The Word Is an Egg*. Ibadan: Kraft Books, 2000, p.38.

*THE POSSIBILITIES OF HOPE

Not long ago, a critic pointed at what he called the "relentless optimism" in my writings. "There is too much hope in your works," he said. "You seem not touched by the ravages of these cynical times." This critic followed up his observation with an assertion that is chilling in its apocalyptic projection. "There's really nothing to laugh about. We are all doomed," he continued, looking more and more like an Old Testament prophet in sackcloth, with an executioner's sword in his hand. That was the critic's first reaction to *Waiting Laughters*, the book which won the award whose presentation provides the occasion for today's address.

This critic's observation was, of course, too grave to be waved aside as the vapid ranting of an avowed cynic. It set me pondering once again about that fragile line between hope and despair, between what was and is, and what is capable of being; between our chronicle of tears and a pageant of laughter waiting, still waiting, at the edge of our lips.

So I knew—and appreciated—the provenance and ambiance of the critic's pessimism, though I refused to be infected by it. For, if we go rigidly by the reality thrust up by the world today, to hope would be to tell a lie, to commit a heinous irrationality, even an unforgivable treachery. At the global level, the world is caught in a crossfire of flux and angst. Old walls have fallen, with new ones rising in their place. Old certitudes have collapsed, supplanted by half-boiled apostasies, more sure, more vehement about the past they have repudiated than the future they anticipate. There is talk about the "new world order," but many are not really sure whose "world" this is, and what is really "new" about it. To complicate matters further, some pundits have climbed to the top of the global rubble, proclaiming what they see as "the end of History."

But History has not even started for Africa (you may say this is an interesting paradox about a continent which cradled the dawn of humankind). For even in this last decade of the twentieth century, Africa still remains the "other" continent, eking out a precarious existence in what, to me, is not just the margin but the margin of the margin. The euphoria of independence of the sixties gave way to the political instability of the seventies, then the economic debacle of the eighties, a decade at the end of which virtually every African country is bankrupt or grossly in debt.

The repercussions of all this for culture, education, and the knowledge industry as a whole are grave and far-reaching. There are fewer schools being built in Africa today than, say, a decade ago: more children are out of school; the indigenous publishing companies which sprang up so enthusiastically about two decades ago have thinned out to a vitiated few. Thanks to massively devalued currencies and unfavorable exchange rates, publishing has become so expensive that books published in Africa are simply unaffordable, while those coming from overseas are priced beyond reach. Thus while computer literacy has become the vogue in other parts of the world, we in Africa still find it difficult to move our populace from A to Z.

There are certainly enough demons here to baffle the spirit, to force those not obstinate enough to throw up their hands in whimpering despondency. But a proper understanding of history will put our present anomy in clearer, if not more bearable, perspective; a more tough-minded dialogue with the past will reveal how much we have gone through, and how far we are capable of going. A philosophy of Africa not informed by historical wisdom is most likely to end in a kind of pessimism born out of prognostication without diagnosis, a sure way of the ontology of defeat.

It is hope which stands at the gate, repelling these demons, empowering our spirit, making sure we do not succumb. This is why, as with Agostinho Neto, that most venerable poet and statesman, hope to me is sacred; it is the guiding principle of my vision, my inalienable companion. Scientists and other wizards of the human body have stipulated how long a human being can live without food, how long without water. No one has told us yet how long a person can live without hope, but we know it must be a very short span indeed. Hope is the nourishment of that vital space which mediates between heart and mind, soul and spirit, a space that is deep, mysterious, and infinitely daring. In it is located the powerhouse of the human psyche, that seat of the vital force which determines the will to live, which translates thought into action. Without hope, life crumbles like a clay doll in the tropical rain; resolve loses its essence and impetus; struggle becomes impossible as the wheel of progress is deprived of its vital hub.

Hope comes in different tones and tenors. There is the politician's hope, a slice of patriotic illusion peddled in the slick, catchy dialect of a salesman. This hope comes alive on noisy campaign grounds or—as is becoming more and more prominent in Africa—in the orders-is-orders constituency of military barracks. This is the kind of hope which builds bridges where there are no rivers, the type which feeds starving crowds with dreams of absent harvests. This is the kind of hope which gives hope a bad name, a hope whose other name is unqualified cynicism.

Counterposed to this is the other kind of hope, a rooted, rugged hope forged from the ore of concrete circumstances, molded by history, toughened in the furnace of contemporary reality. It is an intriguing, problematic hope, ever so conscious of the fragile borders it shares with despair, but possessing enough transcendence, enough visionary resourcefulness always to worst its stubborn foe.

I am a preacher of the gospel of the latter hope. It is a hope inspired and strengthened by the vitality of our people, their resilience, their belief that no matter how similar they may appear to be, no two days end exactly the same way; that no matter how fast the train may run, it will always find the earth ahead, waiting. So when I see the tadpole, I dream a frog; when I see the cloud, I think of rain.

The problems facing Africa today are numerous and daunting but we shall not die in our sleep. Zimbabwe, on whose hallowed soil this speech is being made today, is a testimony to my faith in our ample possibilities. I remember vividly a little over ten years ago when I wrote a poem praising the liberation effort and stressing the inevitability of freedom, a colleague shook his head and described me as starry-eyed. When I met him at a conference about three years ago, he shook that same head in a different direction!

"As long as there is life there is hope," proclaims an old saying. The African situation today responds more appropriately to a reconstructed version of that adage: "As long as there is hope, there is life."

* Acceptance Speech for the Noma Award, Harare, Zimbabwe, 22 August 1991.

INDEX